COMPLETE POEMS OF
FRANCIS THOMPSON

COMPLETE

POEMS OF

FRANCIS

THOMPSON

THE
MODERN LIBRARY
NEW YORK

Random House IS THE PUBLISHER OF

THE MODERN LIBRARY

BENNETT A. CERF · DONALD S. KLOPFER · ROBERT K. HAAS

Manufactured in the United States of America

Printed by Parkway Printing Company   Bound by H. Wolff

DEDICATION OF POEMS

(1893)

To Wilfrid and Alice Meynell

IF the rose in meek duty
   May dedicate humbly
To her grower the beauty
   Wherewith she is comely;
If the mine to the miner
   The jewels that pined in it,
Earth to diviner
   The springs he divined in it;
To the grapes the wine-pitcher
   Their juice that was crushed in it,
Viol to its witcher
   The music lay hushed in it;
If the lips may pay Gladness
   In laughters she wakened,
And the heart to its sadness
   Weeping unslakened,
If the hid and sealed coffer,
   Whose having not his is,
To the loosers may proffer
   Their finding—here this is;
Their lives if all livers
   To the Life of all living,—
To you, O dear givers!
   I give your own giving.

DEDICATION OF POEMS

(1893)

To Wilfrid and Alice Meynell

If the rose in meek duty
    May dedicate humbly
To her grower the beauty
    Wherewith she is comely;
If the mine to the miner
    The jewels that pined in it,
        Earth to diviner;
    The springs he divined in it;
To the grapes the wine-pitcher
    Their juice that was crushed in it,
        Viol to its witcher
    The music lay hushed in it;
If the lips may pay Gladness
    In laughters she waked not,
And the heart to its sadness
    Weeping unslakened,
If the bid and sealed coffer,
    Whose having not his is,
To the loosers may proffer
    Their finding—here, this is;
Their lives it all livers,
    To the Tale of all living,—
To you, O dear givers,
    I give your own giving.

A NOTE BY FRANCIS THOMPSON'S
LITERARY EXECUTOR

In making this Collection I have been governed
by Francis Thompson's express instructions, or
guided by a knowledge of his feelings and pref-
erences acquired during an unbroken intimacy of
nineteen years. His own list of new inclusions and
his own suggested reconsiderations of his formerly
published text have been followed in this edition
of his Poetical Works.

May 1913.   *W. M.*

CONTENTS

CONTENTS

CONTENTS

CONTENTS

CONTENTS

POEMS ON CHILDREN

DAISY

WHERE the thistle lifts a purple crown
   Six foot out of the turf,
And the harebell shakes on the windy hill—
   O breath of the distant surf!—

The hills look over on the South,
   And southward dreams the sea;
And with the sea-breeze hand in hand
   Came innocence and she.

Where 'mid the gorse the raspberry
   Red for the gatherer springs,
Two children did we stray and talk
   Wise, idle, childish things.

She listened with big-lipped surprise,
   Breast-deep mid flower and spine:
Her skin was like a grape whose veins
   Run snow instead of wine.

She knew not those sweet words she spake,
   Nor knew her own sweet way;
But there's never a bird, so sweet a song
   Thronged in whose throat that day.

Oh, there were flowers in Storrington
  On the turf and on the spray;
But the sweetest flower on Sussex hills
  Was the Daisy-flower that day!

Her beauty smoothed earth's furrowed face.
  She gave me tokens three:—
A look, a word of her winsome mouth,
  And a wild raspberry.

A berry red, a guileless look,
  A still word,—strings of sand!
And yet they made my wild, wild heart
  Fly down to her little hand.

For standing artless as the air,
  And candid as the skies,
She took the berries with her hand,
  And the love with her sweet eyes.

The fairest things have fleetest end,
  Their scent survives their close:
But the rose's scent is bitterness
  To him that loved the rose.

She looked a little wistfully,
  Then went her sunshine way:—
The sea's eye had a mist on it,
  And the leaves fell from the day.

She went her unremembering way,
  She went and left in me
The pang of all the partings gone,
  And partings yet to be.

She left me marvelling why my soul
  Was sad that she was glad;
At all the sadness in the sweet,
  The sweetness in the sad.

Still, still I seemed to see her, still
  Look up with soft replies,
And take the berries with her hand,
  And the love with her lovely eyes.

Nothing begins, and nothing ends,
  That is not paid with moan;
For we are born in other's pain,
  And perish in our own.

THE POPPY

To Monica

SUMMER set lip to earth's bosom bare,
And left the flushed print in a poppy there:
Like a yawn of fire from the grass it came,
And the fanning wind puffed it to flapping flame.

With burnt mouth, red like a lion's, it drank
The blood of the sun as he slaughtered sank,
And dipped its cup in the purpurate shine
When the Eastern conduits ran with wine.

Till it grew lethargied with fierce bliss,
And hot as a swinked gipsy is,
And drowsed in sleepy savageries,
With mouth wide a-pout for a sultry kiss.

A child and man paced side by side,
Treading the skirts of eventide;
But between the clasp of his hand and hers
Lay, felt not, twenty withered years.

She turned, with the rout of her dusk South hair,
And saw the sleeping gipsy there:
And snatched and snapped it in swift child's whim,
With—"Keep it, long as you live!"—to him.

And his smile, as nymphs from their laving meres,
Trembled up from a bath of tears;
And joy, like a mew sea-rocked apart,
Tossed on the waves of his troubled heart.

For *he* saw what she did not see,
That—as kindled by its own fervency—
The verge shrivelled inward smoulderingly:
And suddenly 'twixt his hand and hers
He knew the twenty withered years—
No flower, but twenty shrivelled years.

"Was never such thing until this hour,"
Low to his heart he said; "the flower
Of sleep brings wakening to me,
And of oblivion, memory."

"Was never this thing to me," he said,
"Though with bruisèd poppies my feet are red!"
And again to his own heart very low:
"Oh child! I love, for I love and know;

"But you, who love nor know at all
The diverse chambers in Love's guest-hall,
Where some rise early, few sit long:
In how differing accents hear the throng
His great Pentecostal tongue;

"Who know not love from amity,
Nor my reported self from me;
A fair fit gift is this, meseems,
You give—this withering flower of dreams.

"O frankly fickle, and fickly true,
Do you know what the days will do to you?
To your love and you what the days will do,
O frankly fickle, and fickly true?

"You have loved me, Fair, three lives—or days:
'Twill pass with the passing of my face.
But where *I* go, your face goes too,
To watch lest I play false to you.

"I am but, my sweet, your foster-lover,
Knowing well when certain years are over
You vanish from me to another;
Yet I know, and love, like the foster-mother.

"So, frankly fickle, and fickly true!
For my brief life-while I take from you
This token, fair and fit, meseems,
For me—this withering flower of dreams."

The sleep-flower sways in the wheat its head,
Heavy with dreams, as that with bread:
The goodly grain and the sun-flushed sleeper
The reaper reaps, and Time the reaper.

I hang 'mid men my needless head,
And my fruit is dreams, as theirs is bread:
The goodly men and the sun-hazed sleeper
Time shall reap, but after the reaper
The world shall glean of me, me the sleeper.

Love, love! your flower of withered dream
In leavèd rhyme lies safe, I deem,
Sheltered and shut in a nook of rhyme,
From the reaper man, and his reaper Time.

Love! *I* fall into the claws of Time:
But lasts within a leavèd rhyme
All that the world of me esteems—
My withered dreams, my withered dreams.

TO MONICA THOUGHT DYING

You, O the piteous you!
    Who all the long night through
    Anticipatedly
    Disclose yourself to me
    Already in the ways
Beyond our human comfortable days;
    How can you deem what Death
    Impitiably saith
    To me, who listening wake
    For your poor sake?

When a grown woman dies
You know we think unceasingly
What things she said, how sweet, how wise;
And these do make our misery.
    But you were (you to me
The dead anticipatedly!)
You—eleven years, was't not, or so?—
    Were just a child, you know;
And so you never said
Things sweet immeditatably and wise
To interdict from closure my wet eyes:
    But foolish things, my dead, my dead!
    Little and laughable,
    Your age that fitted well.
And was it such things all unmemorable,
    Was it such things could make
Me sob all night for our implacable sake?
    Yet, as you said to me,
In pretty make-believe of revelry,
    So the night long said Death
    With his magniloquent breath;
(And that remembered laughter,
Which in our daily uses followed after,
Was all untuned to pity and to awe:)
    "A cup of chocolate,
    One farthing is the rate,
    You drink it through a straw."

How could I know, how know
Those laughing words when drenched with sobbing so?
Another voice than yours, he hath.
    My dear, was't worth his breath,
His mighty utterance?—yet he saith, and saith!

This dreadful Death to his own dreadfulness
    Doth dreadful wrong,
This dreadful childish babble on his tongue.
That iron tongue made to speak sentences,
And wisdom insupportably complete,
Why should it only say the long night through,
    In mimicry of you,—
    "A cup of chocolate,
    One farthing is the rate,
You drink it through a straw, a straw, a straw!"

    Oh, of all sentences,
    Piercingly incomplete!
Why did you teach that fatal mouth to draw,
    Child, impermissible awe,
    From your old trivialness?
    Why have you done me this
    Most unsustainable wrong,
    And into Death's control
Betrayed the secret places of my soul?—
    Teaching him that his lips,
Uttering their native earthquake and eclipse,
    Could never so avail
To rend from hem to hem the ultimate veil
    Of this most desolate
    Spirit, and leave it stripped and desecrate,—
    Nay, never so have wrung
From eyes and speech weakness unmanned, unmeet,
As when his terrible dotage to repeat
Its little lesson learneth at your feet;
    As when he sits among
    His sepulchres, to play

With broken toys your hand has cast away,
With derelict trinkets of the darling young.
Why have you taught—that he might so complete
    His awful panoply
    From your cast playthings—why,
This dreadful childish babble to his tongue,
    Dreadful and sweet?

THE MAKING OF VIOLA

I

The Father of Heaven.
    Spin, daughter Mary, spin,
    Twirl your wheel with silver din;
    Spin, daughter Mary, spin,
    Spin a tress for Viola.

Angels.

    Spin, Queen Mary, a
    Brown tress for Viola!

II

The Father of Heaven.
    Weave, hands angelical,
    Weave a woof of flesh to pall—
    Weave, hands angelical—
    Flesh to pall our Viola.

Angels.

    Weave, singing brothers, a
    Velvet flesh for Viola!

III

The Father of Heaven.
>   Scoop, young Jesus, for her eyes,
>   Wood-browned pools of Paradise—
>   Young Jesus, for the eyes,
>   For the eyes of Viola.

Angels.
>   Tint, Prince Jesus, a
>   Duskèd eye for Viola!

IV

The Father of Heaven.
>   Cast a star therein to drown,
>   Like a torch in cavern brown,
>   Sink a burning star to drown
>   Whelmed in eyes of Viola.

Angels.
>   Lave, Prince Jesus, a
>   Star in eyes of Viola!

V

The Father of Heaven.
>   Breathe, Lord Paraclete,
>   To a bubbled crystal meet—
>   Breathe, Lord Paraclete—
>   Crystal soul for Viola.

Angels.
>   Breathe, Regal Spirit, a
>   Flashing soul for Viola!

VI

The Father of Heaven.

  Child-angels, from your wings
  Fall the roseal hoverings,
  Child-angels, from your wings,
   On the cheeks of Viola.

Angels.

  Linger, rosy reflex, a
  Quenchless stain, on Viola!

VII

All things being accomplished, saith the Father of Heaven.

  Bear her down, and bearing, sing,
  Bear her down on spyless wing,
  Bear her down, and bearing, sing,
   With a sound of viola.

Angels.

  Music as her name is, a
  Sweet sound of Viola!

VIII

  Wheeling angels, past espial,
  Danced her down with sound of viol;
  Wheeling angels, past espial,
   Descanting on "Viola."

Angels.

  Sing, in our footing, a
  Lovely lilt of "Viola!"

IX

Baby smiled, mother wailed,
Earthward while the sweetling sailed;
Mother smiled, baby wailed,
    When to earth came Viola.

And her elders shall say:
So soon have we taught you a
Way to weep, poor Viola!

X

Smile, sweet baby, smile,
For you will have weeping-while;
Native in your Heaven is smile,—
    But your weeping, Viola?

Whence your smiles we know, but ah!
Whence your weeping, Viola?—
Our first gift to you is a
Gift of tears, my Viola!

TO MY GODCHILD

Francis M. W. M.

THIS labouring, vast, Tellurian galleon,
Riding at anchor off the orient sun,
Had broken its cable, and stood out to space
Down same frore Arctic of the aërial ways:
And now, back warping from the inclement main,
Its vaporous shroudage drenched with icy rain,
It swung into its azure roads again;
When, floated on the prosperous sun-gale, you
Lit, a white halcyon auspice, 'mid our frozen crew.

To the Sun, stranger, surely you belong,
Giver of golden days and golden song;
Nor is it by an all-unhappy plan
You bear the name of me, his constant Magian.
Yet ah! from any other that it came,
Lest fated to my fate you be, as to my name.
When at first those tidings did they bring,
My heart turned troubled at the ominous thing:
Though well may such a title him endower,
For whom a poet's prayer implores a poet's power.
The Assisian, who kept plighted faith to three,
To Song, to Sanctitude, and Poverty,
(In two alone of whom most singers prove
A fatal faithfulness of during love!);
He the sweet Sales, of whom we scarcely ken
How God he could love more, he so loved men;
The crown and crowned of Laura and Italy;
And Fletcher's fellow—from these, and not from me,
Take you your name, and take your legacy!

Or, if a right successive you declare
When worms, or ivies, intertwine my hair,
Take but this Poesy that now followeth
My clayey hest with sullen servile breath,
Made then your happy freedman by testating death.
My song I do but hold for you in trust,
I ask you but to blossom from my dust.
When you have compassed all weak I began,
Diviner poet, and ah! diviner man;
The man at feud with the perduring child
In you before Song's altar nobly reconciled;
From the wise heavens I half shall smile to see
How little a world, which owned you, needed me.

If, while you keep the vigils of the night,
For your wild tears make darkness all too bright,
Some lone orb through your lonely window peeps,
As it played lover over your sweet sleeps;
Think it a golden crevice in the sky,
Which I have pierced but to behold you by!

And when, immortal mortal, droops your head,
And you, the child of deathless song, are dead;
Then, as you search with unaccustomed glance
The ranks of Paradise for my countenance,
Turn not your tread along the Uranian sod
Among the bearded counsellors of God;
For if in Eden as on earth are we,
I sure shall keep a younger company:
Pass where beneath their rangèd gonfalons
The starry cohorts shake their shielded suns,
The dreadful mass of their enridgèd spears;
Pass where majestical the eternal peers,
The stately choice of the great Saintdom, meet—
A silvern segregation, globed complete
In sandalled shadow of the Triune feet;
Pass by where wait, young poet-wayfarer,
Your cousined clusters, emulous to share
With you the roseal lightnings burning 'mid their hair;
Pass the crystalline sea, the Lampads seven:—
Look for me in the nurseries of Heaven.

TO OLIVIA

I FEAR to love thee, Sweet, because
Love's the ambassador of loss;
White flake of childhood, clinging so
To my soiled raiment, thy shy snow
At tenderest touch will shrink and go.
Love me not, delightful child.
My heart, by many snares beguiled,
Has grown timorous and wild.
It would fear thee not at all,
Wert thou not so harmless-small.
Because thy arrows, not yet dire,
Are still unbarbed with destined fire,
I fear thee more than hadst thou stood
Full-panoplied in womanhood.

LITTLE JESUS

*Ex ore infantium, Deus, et lactentium
perfecisti laudem*

LITTLE Jesus, wast Thou shy
Once, and just so small as I?
And what did it feel like to be
Out of Heaven, and just like me?
Didst Thou sometimes think of *there,*
And ask where all the angels were?
I should think that I would cry
For my house all made of sky;
I would look about the air,
And wonder where my angels were;

And at waking 'twould distress me——
Not an angel there to dress me!
Hadst Thou ever any toys,
Like us little girls and boys?
And didst Thou play in Heaven with all
The angels that were not too tall,
With stars for marbles? Did the things
Play *Can you see me?* through their wings?
And did Thy Mother let Thee spoil
Thy robes, with playing on *our* soil?
How nice to have them always new
In Heaven, because 'twas quite clean blue!

Didst Thou kneel at night to pray,
And didst Thou join Thy hands, this way?
And did they tire sometimes, being young,
And make the prayer seem very long?
And dost Thou like it best, that we
Should join our hands to pray to Thee?
I used to think, before I knew,
The prayer not said unless we do.
And did Thy Mother at the night
Kiss Thee, and fold the clothes in right?
And didst Thou feel quite good in bed,
Kissed, and sweet, and Thy prayers said?

Thou canst not have forgotten all
That it feels like to be small:
And Thou know'st I cannot pray
To Thee in my father's way——
When Thou wast so little, say,
Couldst Thou talk Thy Father's way?——

So, a little Child, come down
And hear a child's tongue like Thy own;
Take me by the hand and walk,
And listen to my baby-talk.
To Thy Father show my prayer
(He will look, Thou art so fair),
And say: "O Father, I, Thy Son,
Bring the prayer of a little one."

And He will smile, that children's tongue
Has not changed since Thou wast young!

SISTER SONGS

AN OFFERING TO TWO SISTERS
MONICA & MADELINE (SYLVIA)

THE PROEM

SHREWD winds and shrill—were these the speech of May?
 A ragged, slag-grey sky—invested so,
  Mary's spoilt nursling! wert thou wont to go?
  Or *thou*, Sun-god and song-god, say
Could singer pipe one tiniest linnet-lay,
  While Song did turn away his face from song?
   Or who could be
  In spirit or in body hale for long,—
   Old Æsculap's best Master!—lacking thee?
    At length, then, thou art here!
    On the earth's lethèd ear
  Thy voice of light rings out exultant, strong;
Through dreams she stirs and murmurs at that summons
   dear:
   From its red leash my heart strains tamelessly,
For Spring leaps in the womb of the young year!
   Nay, was it not brought forth before,
    And we waited, to behold it,
    Till the sun's hand should unfold it,
   What the year's young bosom bore?
Even so; it came, nor knew we that it came,

In the sun's eclipse.
　　Yet the birds have plighted vows,
And from the branches piped each other's **name;**
　　　　Yet the season all the boughs
　　　　Has kindled to the finger-tips,—
Mark yonder, how the long laburnum drips
Its jocund spilth of fire, its honey of wild **flame!**
Yea, and myself put on swift quickening,
And answer to the presence of a sudden Spring.

From cloud-zoned pinnacles of the secret spirit
　　Song falls precipitant in dizzying streams;
And, like a mountain-hold when war-shouts stir **it,**
　　The mind's recessèd fastness casts to light
　　Its gleaming multitudes, that from every height
　　　　Unfurl the flaming of a thousand dreams.
Now therefore, thou who bring'st the year to birth,
　　Who guid'st the bare and dabbled feet of May;
Sweet stem to that rose Christ, who from the earth
Suck'st our poor prayers, conveying them to Him;
　　Be aidant, tender Lady, to my lay!
Of thy two maidens somewhat must I say,
Ere shadowy twilight lashes, drooping, dim
　　　　Day's dreamy eyes from us;
　　　　Ere eve has struck and furled
The beamy-textured tent transpicuous,
　　Of webbèd cœrule wrought and woven **calms,**
　　　　Whence has paced forth the lambent-footed **sun.**
And thou disclose my flower of song upcurled,
　　Who from thy fair irradiant palms
Scatterest all love and loveliness as alms;
　　　　Yea, holy one,
Who coin'st thyself to beauty for the world!

Then, Spring's little children, your lauds do ye upraise
To Sylvia, O Sylvia, her sweet, feat ways!
   Your lovesome labours lay away,
   And trick you out in holiday,
      For syllabling to Sylvia;
And all you birds on branches, lave your mouths with May,
   To bear with me this burthen,
      For singing to Sylvia.

PART THE FIRST

THE leaves dance, the leaves sing,
The leaves dance in the breath of the Spring.
   I bid them dance,
   I bid them sing,
   For the limpid glance
   Of my ladyling;
For the gift to the Spring of a dewier spring,
For God's good grace of this ladyling!
I know in the lane, by the hedgerow track,
   The long, broad grasses underneath
Are warted with rain like a toad's knobbed back;
   But here May weareth a rainless wreath.
In the new-sucked milk of the sun's bosom
Is dabbled the mouth of the daisy-blossom;
   The smouldering rosebud chars through its sheath;
The lily stirs her snowy limbs,
      Ere she swims
Naked up through her cloven green,
Like the wave-born Lady of Love Hellene;
And the scattered snowdrop exquisite
      Twinkles and gleams,

As if the showers of the sunny beams
Were splashed from the earth in drops of light.
　　　　Everything
　　　　That is child of Spring
　　Casts its bud or blossoming
Upon the stream of my delight.

Their voices, that scents are, now let them **upraise**
To Sylvia, O Sylvia, her sweet, feat ways;
　　　　Their lovely mother them array,
　　　　And prank them out in holiday,
　　　　　For syllabling to Sylvia;
And all the birds on branches lave their **mouths with May,**
　　　　To bear with me this burthen,
　　　　　For singing to Sylvia.

While thus I stood in mazes bound
　　Of vernal sorcery,
I heard a dainty dubious sound,
　　As of goodly melody;
Which first was faint as if in swound,
　　Then burst so suddenly
In warring concord all around,
That, whence this thing might be,
　　　　To see
The very marrow longed in me!
　　It seemed of air, it seemed of ground,
　　　And never any witchery
Drawn from pipe, or reed, or string,
Made such dulcet ravishing.
'Twas like no earthly instrument,
Yet had something of them all
In its rise, and in its fall;

As if in one sweet consort there were blent
  Those archetypes celestial
Which our endeavouring instruments recall.
So heavenly flutes made murmurous plain
To heavenly viols, that again
—Aching with music—wailed back pain;
Regals release their notes, which rise
Welling, like tears from heart to eyes;
And the harp thrills with thronging sighs.
Horns in mellow flattering
Parley with the cithern-string:—
Hark!—the floating, long-drawn note
Woos the throbbing cithern-string!

Their pretty, pretty prating those citherns sure upraise
For homage unto Sylvia, her sweet, feat ways:
  Those flutes do flute their vowelled lay,
  Their lovely languid language say,
    For lisping to Sylvia;
Those viols' lissom bowings break the heart of May,
  And harps harp their burthen,
    For singing to Sylvia.

Now at that music and that mirth
Rose, as 'twere, veils from earth;
      And I spied
      How beside
Bud, bell, bloom, an elf
Stood, or was the flower itself;
      'Mid radiant air
      All the fair
Frequency swayed in irised wavers.
Some against the gleaming rims

Their bosoms prest
Of the kingcups, to the brims
Filled with sun, and their white limbs
Bathèd in those golden lavers;
Some on the brown, glowing breast
Of that Indian maid, the pansy
(Through its tenuous veils confest
Of swathing light), in a quaint fancy
Tied her knot of yellow favours;
Others dared open draw
Snapdragon's dreadful jaw:
Some, just sprung from out the soil,
Sleeked and shook their rumpled fans
Dropt with sheen
Of moony green;
Others, not yet extricate,
On their hands leaned their weight,
And writhed them free with mickle toil,
Still folded in their veiny vans:
And all with an unsought accord
Sang together from the sward;
Whence had come, and from sprites
Yet unseen, those delights,
As of tempered musics blent,
Which had given me such content.
For haply our best instrument,
Pipe or cithern, stopped or strung,
Mimics but some spirit tongue.

Their amiable voices, I bid them upraise
To Sylvia, O Sylvia, her sweet, feat ways;
  Their lovesome labours laid away,
  To linger out this holiday

In syllabling to Sylvia;
While all the birds on branches lave their mouths with May,
To bear with me this burthen,
For singing to Sylvia.

Next I saw, wonder-whist,
How from the atmosphere a mist,
So it seemed, slow uprist;
And, looking from those elfin swarms,
    I was 'ware
    How the air
Was all populous with forms
Of the Hours, floating down,
Like Nereids through a watery town.
Some, with languors of waved arms,
Fluctuous oared their flexile way;
Some were borne half resupine
On the aërial hyaline,
Their fluid limbs and rare array
Flickering on the wind, as quivers
Trailing weed in running rivers;
And others, in far prospect seen,
Newly loosed on this terrene,
Shot in piercing swiftness came,
With hair a-stream like pale and goblin flame.
As crystálline ice in water,
Lay in air each faint daughter;
Inseparate (or but separate dim)
Circumfused wind from wind-like vest,
Wind-like vest from wind-like limb.
But outward from each lucid breast,
When some passion left its haunt,
Radiate surge of colour came.

Diffusing blush-wise, palpitant,
Dying all the filmy frame.
With some sweet tenderness they would
Turn to an amber-clear and glossy gold;
Or a fine sorrow, lovely to behold,
Would sweep them as the sun and wind's joined flood
  Sweeps a greening-sapphire sea;
  Or they would glow enamouredly
Illustrious sanguine, like a grape of blood;
  Or with mantling poetry
Curd to the tincture which the opal hath.
Like rainbows thawing in a moonbeam bath.
So paled they, flushed they, swam they, sang melodiously.

Their chanting, soon fading, let them, too, upraise
For homage unto Sylvia, her sweet, feat rays;
  Weave with suave float their wavèd way,
  And colours take of holiday,
    For syllabling to Sylvia;
And all the birds on branches lave their mouths with May,
  To bear with me this burthen,
    For singing to Sylvia.

Then, through those translucencies,
As grew my senses clearer clear,
Did I see, and did I hear,
How under an elm's canopy
Wheeled a flight of Dryades
Murmuring measured melody.
Gyre in gyre their treading was,
Wheeling with an adverse flight,
In twi-circle o'er the grass,
These to left, and those to right;

All the band
Linkèd by each other's hand;
Decked in raiment stainèd as
The blue-helmèd aconite.
And they advance with flutter, with grace,
    To the dance,
Moving on with a dainty pace,
As blossoms mince it on river swells.
Over their heads their cymbals shine,
Round each ankle gleams a twine
    Of twinkling bells—
Tune twirled golden from their cells.
Every step was a tinkling sound,
As they glanced in their dancing-ground.
Clouds in cluster with such a sailing
Float o'er the light of the wasting moon,
As the cloud of their gliding veiling
Swung in the sway of the dancing-tune.
There was the clash of their cymbals clanging,
Ringing of swinging bells clinging their feet;
And the clang on wing it seemed a-hanging,
Hovering round their dancing so fleet.—
I stirred, I rustled more than meet;
Whereat they broke to the left and right,
With eddying robes like aconite
    Blue of helm;
And I beheld to the foot o' the elm.

They have not tripped those dances, betrayed to my gaze,
To glad the heart of Sylvia, beholding of their maze;
    Through barky walls have slid away,
    And tricked them in their holiday,
        For other than for Sylvia;

While all the birds on branches lave their mouths with May,
  And bear with me this burthen,
    For singing to Sylvia.

Where its umbrage was enrooted,
    Sat, white-suited,
Sat, green-amiced and bare-footed,
    Spring, amid her minstrelsy;
There she sat amid her ladies,
    Where the shade is
Sheen as Enna mead ere Hades'
    Gloom fell 'thwart Persephone.
Dewy buds were interstrown
Through her tresses hanging down,
    And her feet
    Were most sweet,
Tinged like sea-stars, rosied brown.
A throng of children like to flowers were sown
About the grass beside, or clomb her knee:
I looked who were that favoured company.
    And one there stood
    Against the beamy flood
Of sinking day, which, pouring its abundance,
Sublimed the illuminous and volute redundance
Of locks that, half dissolving, floated round her face;
    As see I might
Far off a lily-cluster poised in sun
    Dispread its gracile curls of light.
I knew what chosen child was there in place!
I knew there might no brows be, save of one,
With such Hesperian fulgence compassèd,
Which in her moving seemed to wheel about her head.

O Spring's little children, more loud your lauds upraise,
For this is even Sylvia, with her sweet, feat ways!
  Your lovesome labours lay away,
  And prank you out in holiday,
    For syllabling to Sylvia;
And all you birds on branches, lave your mouths with May,
  To bear with me this burthen,
    For singing to Sylvia!

Spring, goddess, is it thou, desirèd long?
And art thou girded round with this young train?—
If ever I did do thee ease in song,
Now of thy grace let me one meed obtain,
    And list thou to one plain.
      Oh, keep still in thy train,
After the years when others therefrom fade,
    This tiny, well-belovèd maid!
To whom the gate of my heart's fortalice,
    With all which in it is,
And the shy self who doth therein immew him
'Gainst what loud leaguerers battailously woo him,
      I, bribèd traitor to him,
        Set open for one kiss.

Then suffer, Spring, thy children, that lauds they should
      upraise
To Sylvia, this Sylvia, her sweet, feat ways;
  Their lovely labours lay away,
  And trick them out in holiday,
    For syllabling to Sylvia;
And that all birds on branches lave their mouths with May,
  To bear with me this burthen,
    For singing to Sylvia.

A kiss? for a child's kiss?
Aye, goddess, even for this.
Once, bright Sylviola, in days not far,
Once—in that nightmare-time which still doth haunt
My dreams, a grim, unbidden visitant—
Forlorn, and faint, and stark,
I had endured through watches of the dark
The abashless inquisition of each star,
Yea, was the outcast mark
Of all those heavenly passers' scrutiny;
Stood bound and helplessly
For Time to shoot his barbèd minutes at me;
Suffered the trampling hoof of every hour
In night's slow-wheelèd car;
Until the tardy dawn dragged me at length
From under those dread wheels; and, bled of strength,
I waited the inevitable last.
Then there came past
A child; like thee, a spring-flower; but a flower
Fallen from the budded coronal of Spring,
And through the city-streets blown withering.
She passed,—O brave, sad, lovingest, tender thing!
And of her own scant pittance did she give,
That I might eat and live:
Then fled, a swift and trackless fugitive.
Therefore I kissed in thee
The heart of Childhood, so divine for me;
And her, through what sore ways,
And what unchildish days,
Borne from me now, as then, a trackless fugitive.
Therefore I kissed in thee
Her, child! and innocency,
And spring, and all things that have gone from me,

'And that shall never be;
All vanished hopes, and all most hopeless bliss,
    Came with thee to my kiss.
And ah! so long myself had strayed afar
From child, and woman, and the boon earth's green,
And all wherewith life's face is fair beseen;
    Journeying its journey bare
Five suns, except of the all-kissing sun
      Unkissed of one;
      Almost I had forgot
      The healing harms,
And whitest witchery, a-lurk in that
Authentic cestus of two girdling arms:
      And I remembered not
    The subtle sanctities which dart
From childish lips' unvalued precious brush,
Nor how it makes the sudden lilies push
   Between the loosening fibres of the heart.
      Then, that thy little kiss
      Should be to me all this,
Let workaday wisdom blink sage lids thereat;
Which towers a flight three hedgerows high, poor bat!
   And straightway charts me out the empyreal air.
Its chart I wing not by, its canon of worth
Scorn not, nor reck though mine should breed it mirth:
And howso thou and I may be disjoint,
Yet still my falcon spirit makes her point
      Over the covert where
Thou, sweetest quarry, hast put in from her!

(*Soul, hush these sad numbers, too sad to upraise*
In hymning bright Sylvia, unlearn'd in such ways!
   Our mournful moods lay we away,

And prank our thoughts in holiday,
For syllabling to Sylvia;
When all the birds on branches lave their mouths with May,
To bear with us this burthen,
For singing to Sylvia!)

Then thus Spring, bounteous lady, made reply:
'O lover of me and all my progeny,
For grace to you
I take her ever to my retinue.
Over thy form, dear child, alas! my art
Cannot prevail; but mine immortalizing
Touch I lay upon thy heart.
Thy soul's fair shape
In my unfading mantle's green I drape,
And thy white mind shall rest by my devising
A Gideon-fleece amid life's dusty drouth.
If Even burst yon globèd yellow grape
(Which is the sun to mortals' sealèd sight)
Against her stainèd mouth;
Or if white-handed light
Draw thee yet dripping from the quiet pools,
Still lucencies and cools,
Of sleep, which all night mirror constellate dreams;
Like to the sign which led the Israelite,
Thy soul, through day or dark,
A visible brightness on the chosen ark
Of thy sweet body and pure,
Shall it assure,
With auspice large and tutelary gleams,
Appointed solemn courts, and covenanted streams.'

Cease, Spring's little children, now cease your lauds to raise;
That dream is past, and Sylvia, with her sweet, feat ways.
  Our lovèd labour, laid away,
    Is smoothly ended; said our say,
      Our syllabling to Sylvia.
Make sweet, you birds on branches! make sweet your mouths
  with May!
      But borne is this burthen,
        Sung unto Sylvia.

PART THE SECOND

And now, thou elder nursling of the nest;
    Ere all the intertangled west
      Be one magnificence
Of multitudinous blossoms that o'errun
The flaming brazen bowl o' the burnished sun
      Which they do flower from,
How shall I 'stablish *thy* memorial?
Nay, how or with what countenance shall I come
      To plead in my defence
      For loving thee at all?
I who can scarcely speak my fellows' speech,
Love their love, or mine own love to them teach;
A bastard barred from their inheritance,
  Who seem, in this dim shape's uneasy nook,
Some sun-flower's spirit which by luckless chance
  Has mournfully its tenement mistook;
When it were better in its right abode,
Heartless and happy lackeying its god.
How com'st thou, little tender thing of white,
Whose very touch full scantly me beseems,

How com'st thou resting on my vaporous dreams,
   Kindling a wraith there of earth's vernal green?
      Even so as I have seen,
   In night's aërial sea with no wind blust'rous,
'A ribbèd tract of cloudy malachite
      Curve a shored crescent wide;
'And on its slope marge shelving to the night
   The stranded moon lay quivering like a lustrous
      Medusa newly washed up from the tide,
Lay in an oozy pool of its own deliquious light.
   Yet hear how my excuses may prevail,
      Nor, tender white orb, be thou opposite!
Life and life's beauty only hold their revels
In the abysmal ocean's luminous levels.
There, like the phantasms of a poet pale,
   The exquisite marvels sail:
Clarified silver; greens and azures frail
As if the colours sighed themselves away,
And blent in supersubtile interplay
   As if they swooned into each other's arms;
      Repured vermilion,
      Like ear-tips 'gainst the sun;
And beings that, under night's swart pinion,
Make every wave upon the harbour-bars
      A beaten yolk of stars.
But where day's glance turns baffled from the deeps,
      Die out those lovely swarms;
'And in the immense profound no creature glides or creeps.

Love and love's beauty only hold their revels
In life's familiar, penetrable levels:
      What of its ocean-floor?
      I dwell there evermore.

From almost earliest youth
I raised the lids o' the truth,
And forced her bend on me her shrinking sight;
Ever I knew me Beauty's eremite,
In antre of this lowly body set,
Girt with a thirsty solitude of soul.
Natheless I not forget
How I have, even as the anchorite,
I too, imperishing essences that console.
Under my ruined passions, fallen and sere,
The wild dreams stir, like little radiant girls
Whom in the moulted plumage of the year
Their comrades sweet have buried to the curls.
Yet, though their dedicated amorist,
How often do I bid my visions hist,
Deaf to them, pleading all their piteous fills;
Who weep, as weep the maidens of the mist
Clinging the necks of the unheeding hills:
And their tears wash them lovelier than before,
That from grief's self our sad delight grows more.
Fair are the soul's uncrispèd calms, indeed,
Endiapered with many a spiritual form
Of blosmy-tinctured weed;
But scarce itself is conscious of the store
Suckled by it, and only after storm
Casts up its loosened thoughts upon the shore.
To this end my deeps are stirred;
And I deem well why life unshared
Was ordainèd me of yore.
In pairing-time, we know, the bird
Kindles to its deepmost splendour,
And the tender
Voice is tenderest in its throat:

Were its love, for ever nigh it,
 Never by it,
 It might keep a vernal note,
The crocean and amethystine
 In their pristine
 Lustre linger on its coat.
Therefore must my song-bower lone be,
 That my tone be
 Fresh with dewy pain alway;
She, who scorns my dearest care ta'en,
 An uncertain
 Shadow of the sprite of May.
And is my song sweet, as they say?
'Tis sweet for one whose voice has no reply,
 Save silence's sad cry:
And are its plumes a burning bright array?
They burn for an unincarnated eye.
A bubble, charioteered by the inward breath
 Which, ardorous for its own invisible lure,
Urges me glittering to aërial death,
 I am rapt towards that bodiless paramour;
Blindly the uncomprehended tyranny
 Obeying of my heart's impetuous might.
 The earth and all its planetary kin,
Starry buds tangled in the whirling hair
That flames round the Phœbean wassailer,
 Speed no more ignorant, more predestined flight,
 Than I, *her* viewless tresses netted in.
As some most beautiful one, with lovely taunting,
Her eyes of guileless guile o'ercanopies,
 Does her hid visage bow,
And miserly your covetous gaze allow,
 By inchmeal, coy degrees,

Saying—'Can you see me now?'
Yet from the mouth's reflex you guess the wanting
Smile of the coming eyes
In all their upturned grievous witcheries,
Before that sunbreak rise;
And each still hidden feature view within
Your mind, as eager scrutinies detail
The moon's young rondure through the shamefast veil
Drawn to her gleaming chin:
After this wise,
From the enticing smile of earth and skies
I dream my unknown Fair's refusèd gaze;
And guessingly her love's close traits devise,
Which she with subtile coquetries
Through little human glimpses slow displays,
Cozening my mateless days
By sick, intolerable delays.
And so I keep mine uncompanioned ways;
And so my touch, to golden poesies
Turning love's bread, is bought at hunger's price.
So,—in the inextinguishable wars
Which roll song's Orient on the sullen night
Whose ragged banners in their own despite
Take on the tinges of the hated light,—
So Sultan Phœbus has his Janizars.
But if mine unappeasèd cicatrices
Might get them lawful ease;
Were any gentle passion hallowed me,
Who must none other breath of passion feel
Save such as winnows to the fledgèd heel
The tremulous Paradisal plumages;
The conscious sacramental trees
Which ever be

Shaken celestially,
Consentient with enamoured wings, might know my love for
    thee.
. Yet is there more, whereat none guesseth, love!
    Upon the ending of my deadly night
(Whereof thou hast not the surmise, and slight
Is all that any mortal knows thereof),
    Thou wert to me that earnest of day's light,
When, like the back of a gold-mailèd saurian
    Heaving its slow length from Nilotic slime,
The first long gleaming fissure runs Aurorian
    Athwart the yet dun firmament of prime.
Stretched on the margin of the cruel sea
        Whence they had rescued me,
    With faint and painful pulses was I lying;
        Not yet discerning well
If I had 'scaped, or were an icicle,
        Whose thawing is its dying.
Like one who sweats before a despot's gate,
Summoned by some presaging scroll of fate,
And knows not whether kiss or dagger wait;
And all so sickened is his countenance,
The courtiers buzz, 'Lo, doomed!' and look at him
        askance:—
        At Fate's dread portal then
        Even so stood I, I ken,
Even so stood I, between a joy and fear,
And said to mine own heart, 'Now if the end be here!'

They say, Earth's beauty seems completest
    To them that on their death-beds rest;
Gentle lady! she smiles sweetest
    Just ere she clasps us to her breast.

And I,—now *my* Earth's countenance grew bright,
Did she but smile me towards that nuptial-night?
But, whileas on such dubious bed I lay,
   One unforgotten day,
  As a sick child waking sees
   Wide-eyed daisies
  Gazing on it from its hand,
  Slipped there for its dear amazes;
  So between thy father's knees
   I saw *thee* stand,
   And through my hazes
Of pain and fear thine eyes' young wonder shone.
Then, as flies scatter from a carrion,
 Or rooks in spreading gyres like broken smoke
 Wheel, when some sound their quietude has broke,
Fled, at thy countenance, all that doubting spawn:
 The heart which I had questioned spoke,
A cry impetuous from its depth was drawn,—
'I take the omen of this face of dawn!'
And with the omen to my heart cam'st thou.
  Even with a spray of tears
That one light draft was fixed there for the years.

   And now?—
The hours I tread ooze memories of thee, Sweet,
  Beneath my casual feet.
  With rainfall as the lea,
  The day is drenched with thee;
 In little exquisite surprises
Bubbling deliciousness of thee arises
  From sudden places,
  Under the common traces
Of my most lethargied and customed paces.

As an Arab journeyeth
Through a sand of Ayaman,
Lean Thirst, lolling its cracked tongue,
Lagging by his side along;
And a rusty-wingèd Death
Grating its low flight before,
Casting ribbèd shadows o'er
The blank desert, blank and tan:
He lifts by hap toward where the morning's roots are
        His weary stare,—
    Sees, although they plashless mutes are,
        Set in a silver air
    Fountains of gelid shoots are,
        Making the daylight fairest fair;
    Sees the palm and tamarind
Tangle the tresses of a phantom wind;—
A sight like innocence when one has sinned!
A green and maiden freshness smiling there,
        While with unblinking glare
The tawny-hided desert crouches watching her.

        'Tis a vision:
    Yet the greeneries Elysian
He has known in tracts afar;
Thus the enamouring fountains flow,
Those the very palms that grow,
By rare-gummed Sava, or Herbalimar.—
    Such a watered dream has tarried
    Trembling on my desert arid;
        Even so
    Its lovely gleamings
        Seemings show
    Of things not seemings;

And I gaze,
Knowing that, beyond my ways,
Verily
All these *are*, for these are She.

Eve no gentlier lays her cooling cheek
On the burning brow of the sick earth,
Sick with death, and sick with birth,
Aeon to aeon, in secular fever twirled,
Than thy shadow soothes this weak
And distempered being of mine.
In all I work, my hand includeth thine;
Thou rushest down in every stream
Whose passion frets my spirit's deepening gorge;
Unhood'st mine eyas-heart, and fliest my dream;
Thou swing'st the hammers of my forge;
As the innocent moon, that nothing does but shine,
Moves all the labouring surges of the world.

Pierce where thou wilt the springing thought in me,
And there thy pictured countenance lies enfurled,
As in the cut fern lies the imaged tree.
This poor song that sings of thee,
This fragile song, is but a curled
Shell outgathered from thy sea,
And murmurous still of its nativity.
Princess of Smiles,
Sorceress of most unlawful-lawful wiles,
Cunning pit for gazers' senses,
Overstrewn with innocences!
Purities gleam white like statues
In the fair lakes of thine eyes,
And I watch the sparkles that use
There to rise,

Knowing these
Are bubbles from the calyces
Of the lovely thoughts that breathe
Paving, like water-flowers, thy spirit's floor beneath.

O thou most dear!
Who art thy sex's complex harmony
God-set more facilely;
To thee may love draw near
Without one blame or fear,
Unchidden save by his humility:
Thou Perseus' Shield wherein I view secure
The mirrored Woman's fateful-fair allure!
Whom Heaven still leaves a twofold dignity,
As girlhood gentle, and as boyhood free;
With whom no most diaphanous webs enwind
The barèd limbs of the rebukeless mind.
Wild Dryad, all unconscious of thy tree,
With which indissolubly
The tyrannous time shall one day make thee whole;
Whose frank arms pass unfretted through its bole;
Who wear'st thy femineity
Light as entrailèd blossoms, that shalt find
It erelong silver shackles unto thee:
Thou whose young sex is yet but in thy soul;—
As hoarded in the vine
Hang the gold skins of undelirious wine,
As air sleeps, till it toss its limbs in breeze;—
In whom the mystery which lures and sunders,
Grapples and thrusts apart, endears, estranges,
—The dragon to its own Hesperides—
Is gated under slow-revolving changes,
Manifold doors of heavy-hingèd years:—

So once, ere Heaven's eyes were filled with wonders
　　To see Laughter rise from Tears,
　　Lay in beauty not yet mighty,
　　　　Conchèd in translucencies,
　　The antenatal Aphrodite,
Caved magically under magic seas;
Caved dreamlessly beneath the dreamful seas.

　　　　'Whose sex is in thy soul!'
　　　　What think we of thy soul?
　　Which has no parts, and cannot grow,
　　Unfurled not from an embryo;
Born of full stature, lineal to control;
And yet a pigmy's yoke must undergo:
Yet must keep pace and tarry, patient, kind,
With its unwilling scholar, the dull, tardy mind;
Must be obsequious to the body's powers,
Whose low hands mete its paths, set ope and close its ways;
　　　　Must do obeisance to the days,
And wait the little pleasure of the hours;
　　　　Yea, ripe for kingship, yet must be
Captive in statuted minority!
So is all power fulfilled, as soul in thee.
So still the ruler by the ruled takes rule,
And wisdom weaves itself i' the loom o' the fool.
The splendent sun no splendour can display
Till on gross things he dash his broken ray,
From cloud and tree and flower re-tossed in prismy spray.
Did not obstruction's vessel hem it in,
Force were not force, would spill itself in vain;
We know the Titan by his champèd chain.
Stay is neat's cradle, it is rocked therein,
And by check's hand is burnished into light;

If hate were none, would love burn lowlier bright?
God's Fair were guessed scarce but for opposite sin;
Yea, and His Mercy, I do think it well,
Is flashed back from the brazen gates of Hell.
　　　The heavens decree
All power fulfil itself as soul in thee.
For supreme Spirit subject was to clay,
　　And Law from its own servants learned a law,
And Light besought a lamp unto its way,
　　　And Awe was reined in awe,
　　　At one small house of Nazareth;
　　　　And Golgotha
Saw Breath to breathlessness resign its breath,
And Life do homage for its crown to death.

So is all power, as soul in thee, increased!
　　But, knowing this, in knowledge's despite
　　I fret against the law severe that stains
　　　Thy spirit with eclipse;
When—as a nymph's carven head sweet water drips,
　　For others oozing so the cool delight
　　Which cannot steep her stiffened mouth of stone—
Thy nescient lips repeat maternal strains.
　　　Memnonian lips!
Smitten with singing from thy mother's East,
　　And murmurous with music not their own:
　　Nay, the lips flexile, while the mind alone
　　　A passionless statue stands.
　　　Oh, pardon, innocent one!
　　Pardon at thine unconscious hands!
'Murmurous with music not their own,' I say?
And in that saying how do I missay,
　　　When from the common sands

Of poorest common speech of common day
Thine accents sift the golden musics out!
    And ah, we poets, I misdoubt,
      Are little more than thou!
We speak a lesson taught we know not how,
    And what it is that from us flows
The hearer better than the utterer knows.

      Thou canst foreshape thy word;
      The poet is not lord
    Of the next syllable may come
    With the returning pendulum;
And what he plans to-day in song,
To-morrow sings it in another tongue.
    Where the last leaf fell from his bough,
    He knows not if a leaf shall grow;
    Where he sows he doth not reap,
    He reapeth where he did not sow;
    He sleeps, and dreams forsake his sleep
    To meet him on his waking way.
Vision will mate him not by law and vow:
    Disguised in life's most hodden-grey,
By the most beaten road of everyday
She waits him, unsuspected and unknown.
      The hardest pang whereon
He lays his mutinous head may be a Jacob's stone.
In the most iron crag his foot can tread
    A Dream may strew her bed,
    And suddenly his limbs entwine,
And draw him down through rock as sea-nymphs might
    through brine.
But, unlike those feigned temptress-ladies who
In guerdon of a night the lover slew,

When the embrace has failed, the rapture fled,
Not he, not he, the wild sweet witch is dead!
  And though he cherisheth
The babe most strangely born from out her death,
Some tender trick of her it hath, maybe,—
   It is not she!

Yet, even as the air is rumorous of fray
 Before the first shafts of the sun's onslaught
  From gloom's black harness splinter,
  And Summer move on Winter
With the trumpet of the March, and the pennon of the
  May;
  As gesture outstrips thought;
So haply, toyer with ethereal strings,
Are thy blind repetitions of high things
The murmurous gnats whose aimless hoverings
  Reveal song's summer in the air;
The outstretched hand, which cannot thought declare,
  Yet is thought's harbinger.
These strains the way for thine own strains prepare;
We feel the music moist upon this breeze,
And hope the congregating poesies.
  Sundered yet by thee from us
  Wait, with wild eyes luminous,
All thy winged things that are to be;
They flit against thee, Gate of Ivory!
They clamour on the portress Destiny,—
'Set her wide, so we may issue through,
Our vans are quick for that they have to do!'
  Suffer still your young desire;
Your plumes but bicker at the tips with fire;
Tarry their kindling—they will beat the higher.

And thou, bright girl, not long shalt thou repeat
Idly the music from thy mother caught;
    Not vainly has she wrought,
Not vainly from the cloudward-jetting turret
Of her aërial mind for thy weak feet
Let down the silken ladder of her thought.
    She bare thee with a double pain,
      Of the body and the spirit;
    Thou thy fleshly weeds hast ta'en,
      Thy diviner weeds inherit!
The precious streams which through thy young lips roll
Shall leave their lovely delta in thy soul:
    Where sprites of so essential kind
      Set their paces,
    Surely they shall leave behind
      The green traces
    Of their sportance in the mind;
    And thou shalt, ere we well may know it,
      Turn that daintiness, a poet,—
        Elfin-ring
    Where sweet fancies foot and sing.
    So it may be, so it *shall* be,—
    Oh, take the prophecy from me!
What if the old fastidious sculptor, Time,
    This crescent marvel of his hands
    Carveth all too painfully,
And I who prophesy shall never see?
What if the niche of its predestined rhyme,
    Its aching niche, too long expectant stands?
      Yet shall he after sore delays
      On some exultant day of days
      The white enshrouding childhood raise
From thy fair spirit, finished for our gaze;

While we (but 'mongst that happy 'we'
    The prophet cannot be!)—
While we behold with no astonishments,
With that serene fulfilment of delight
        Wherewith we view the sight
    When the stars pitch the golden tents
Of their high campment on the plains of night.
Why should amazement be our satellite?
        What wonder in such things?
If angels have hereditary wings,
    If not by Salic law is handed down
        The poet's crown,
    To thee, born in the purple of the throne,
        The laurel must belong:
        Thou, in thy mother's right
Descendant of Castalian-chrismèd kings—
    O Princess of the Blood of Song!

Peace! Too impetuously have I been winging
    Toward vaporous heights wnich beckon and beguile.
    I sink back, saddened to my inmost mind;
Even as I list a-dream that mother singing
    The poesy of sweet tone, and sadden while
        Her voice is cast in troubled wake behind
        The keel of her keen spirit. Thou art enshrined
In a too primal innocence for this eye—
Intent on such untempered radiancy—
Not to be pained; my clay can scarce endure
Ungrieved the effluence near of essences so pure.
        Therefore, little tender maiden,
        Never be thou overshaden
        With a mind whose canopy
        Would shut out the sky from thee;

Whose tangled branches intercept Heaven's light:
    I will not feed my unpastured heart
    On thee, green pleasaunce as thou art,
To lessen by one flower thy happy daisies white.
The water-rat is earth-hued like the runlet
    Whereon he swims; and how in me should lurk
Thoughts apt to neighbour thine, thou creature sunlit?
      If through long fret and irk
Thine eyes within their browed recesses were
Worn caves where thought lay couchant in its lair;
Wert thou a spark among dank leaves, ah ruth!
With age in all thy veins, while all thy heart was youth;
    Our contact might run smooth.
But life's Eoan dews still moist thy ringèd hair;
    Dian's chill finger-tips
Thaw if at night they happen on thy lips;
The flying fringes of the sun's cloak frush
'The fragile leaves which on those warm lips blush;
    And joy only lurks retirèd
    In the dim gloaming of thine irid.
Then since my love drags this poor shadow, me,
And one without the other may not be,
    From both I guard thee free.
    It still is much, yes, it is much,
Only—my dream!—to love my love of thee;
    And it is much, yes, it is much,
In hands which thou hast touched to feel thy touch,
In voices which have mingled with thine own
    To hear a double tone.
As anguish, for supreme expression prest,
    Borrows its saddest tongue from jest,
    Thou hast of absence so create
    A presence more importunate;

And thy voice pleads its sweetest suit
    When it is mute.
I thank the once accursèd star
    Which did me teach
To make of Silence my familiar,
Who hath the rich reversion of thy speech,
Since the most charming sounds thy thoughts can wear,
Cast off, fall to that pale attendant's share;
    And thank the gift which made my mind
A shadow-world, wherethrough the shadows wind
Of all the loved and lovely of my kind.

    Like a maiden Saxon, folden,
      As she flits, in moon-drenched mist;
    Whose curls streaming flaxen-golden,
      By the misted moonbeams kist,
    Dispread their filmy floating silk
      Like honey steeped in milk:
    So, vague goldenness remote,
    Through my thoughts I watch thee float.
When the snake summer casts her blazoned skin
We find it at the turn of autumn's path,
And think it summer that rewinded hath,
    Joying therein;
And this enamouring slough of thee, thine elf,
    I take it for thyself;
Content. Content? Yea, title it content.
The very loves that belt thee must prevent
My love, I know, with their legitimacy:
As the metallic vapours, that are swept
Athwart the sun, in his light intercept
    The very hues
Which their conflagrant elements effuse.

But, my love, my heart, my fair,
That only I should see thee rare,
Or tent to the hid core thy rarity,—
This were a mournfulness more piercing far
Than that those other loves my own must bar,
Or thine for others leave thee none for me.

But on a day whereof I think,
One shall dip his hand to drink
In that still water of thy soul,
And its imaged tremors race
Over thy joy-troubled face,
As the intervolved reflections roll
From a shaken fountain's brink,
With swift light wrinkling its alcove.
From the hovering wing of Love
The warm stain shall flit roseal on thy cheek.
Then, sweet blushet! whenas he,
The destined paramount of thy universe,
Who has no worlds to sigh for, ruling thee,
Ascends his vermeil throne of empery,
One grace alone I seek.
Oh! may this treasure-galleon of my verse,
Fraught with its golden passion, oared with cadent rhyme,
Set with a towering press of fantasies,
Drop safely down the time,
Leaving mine islèd self behind it far
Soon to be sunken in the abysm of seas
(As down the years the splendour voyages
From some long ruined and night-submergèd star),
And in thy subject sovereign's havening heart
Anchor the freightage of its virgin ore;
Adding its wasteful mote

To his own overflowing treasury.
So through his river mine shall reach thy sea,
      Bearing its confluent part;
      In his pulse mine shall thrill;
And the quick heart shall quicken from the heart that's
    still.

Ah, help, my Dæmon, that hast served me well!
      Not at this last, oh, do not me disgrace!
      I faint, I sicken, darkens all my sight,
      As, poised upon this unprevisioned height,
        I lift into its place
The utmost aery traceried pinnacle.
So; it is builded, the high tenement,
      —God grant!—to mine intent:
Most like a palace of the Occident,
      Up-thrusting, toppling maze on maze,
        Its mounded blaze,
And washèd by the sunset's rosy waves,
Whose sea drinks rarer hue from those rare walls it
    laves.
      Yet wail, my spirits, wail!
So few therein to enter shall prevail.
Scarce fewer could win way, if their desire
A dragon baulked, with involuted spire,
And writhen snout spattered with yeasty fire.
For at the elfin portal hangs a horn
      Which none can wind aright
      Save the appointed knight
Whose lids the fay-wings brushed when he was born.
      All others stray forlorn,
Or glimpsing, through the blazoned windows scrolled.
Receding labyrinths lessening tortuously

In half obscurity;
With mystic images, inhuman, cold,
That flameless torches hold.
But who can wind that horn of migh'
(The horn of dead Heliades) aright,—
Straight
Open for him shall roll the conscious gate;
And light leap up from all the torches there,
And life leap up in every torchbearer,
And the stone faces kindle in the glow,
And into the blank eyes the irids grow,
And through the dawning irids ambushed meanings show.
Illumined this wise on,
He threads securely the far intricacies,
With brede from Heaven's wrought vesture overstrewn;
Swift Tellus' purfled tunic, girt upon
With the blown chlamys of her fluttering seas;
And the freaked kirtle of the pearlèd moon:
Until he gain the structure's core, where stands—
A toil of magic hands—
The unbodied spirit of the sorcerer,
Most strangely rare,
As is a vision remembered in the noon;
Unbodied, yet to mortal seeing clear,
Like sighs exhaled in eager atmosphere.
From human haps and mutabilities
It rests exempt, beneath the edifice
To which itself gave rise;
Sustaining centre to the bubble of stone
Which, breathed from it, exists by it alone.
Yea, ere Saturnian earth her child consumes,
And I lie down with outworn ossuaries,
Ere death's grim tongue anticipates the tomb's

Siste viator, in this storied urn
My living heart is laid to throb and burn,
Till end be ended, and till ceasing cease.

And thou by whom this strain hath parentage;
Wantoner between the yet untreacherous claws
Of newly-whelped existence! ere he pause,
What gift to thee can yield the archimage?
For coming seasons' frets
What aids, what amulets,
What softenings, or what brightenings?
As Thunder writhes the lash of his long lightnings
About the growling heads of the brute main
Foaming at mouth, until it wallow again
In the scooped oozes of its bed of pain;
So all the gnashing jaws, the leaping heads
Of hungry menaces, and of ravening dreads,
Of pangs
Twitch-lipped, with quivering nostrils and immitigate fangs
I scourge beneath the torment of my charms
That their repentless nature fear to work thee harms.
And as yon Apollonian harp-player,
Yon wandering psalterist of the sky,
With flickering strings which scatter melody,
The silver-stolèd damsels of the sea,
Or lake, or fount, or stream,
Enchants from their ancestral heaven of waters
To Naiad it through the unfrothing air;
My song enchants so out of undulous dream
The glimmering shapes of its dim-tressèd daughters
And missions each to be thy minister,
Saying: 'O ye,
The organ-stops of being's harmony;

The blushes on existence's pale face,
          Lending it sudden grace;
Without whom we should but guess Heaven's worth
By blank negations of this sordid earth
          (So haply to the blind may light
Be but gloom's undetermined opposite);
Ye who are thus as the refracting air
Whereby we see Heaven's sun before it rise
Above the dull line of our mortal skies;
As breathing on the strainèd ear that sighs
From comrades viewless unto strainèd eyes,
Soothing our terrors in the lampless night;
Ye who can make this world, where all is deeming,
What world ye list, being arbiters of seeming;
Attend upon her ways, benignant powers!
Unroll ye life a carpet for her feet,
And cast ye down before them blossomy hours,
Until her going shall be clogged with sweet!
All dear emotions whose new-bathèd hair,
Still streaming from the soul, in love's warm air
Smokes with a mist of tender fantasies;
          All these,
And all the heart's wild growths which, swiftly bright,
Spring up the crimson agarics of a night,
No pain in withering, yet a joy arisen;
And all thin shapes more exquisitely rare,
          More subtly fair,
Than these weak ministering words have spell to prison
Within the magic circle of this rhyme;
And all the fays who in our creedless clime
          Have sadly ceased,
Bearing to other children childhood's proper feast;
Whose robes are fluent crystal, crocus-hued,

Whose wings are wind a-fire, whose mantles wrought
From spray that falling rainbows shake to air;
These, ye familiars to my wizard thought,
Make things of journal custom unto her;
  With lucent feet imbrued,
  If young Day tread, a glorious vintager,
The wine-press of the purple-foamèd east;
Or round the nodding sun, flush-faced and sunken,
  His wild Bacchantes drunken
Reel, with rent woofs a-flaunt, their westering rout.'

—But lo! at length the day is lingered out,
At length my Ariel lays his viol by;
We sing no more to thee, child, he and I;
  The day is lingered out:
    In slow wreaths folden
    Around yon censer, spherèd, golden,
    Vague Vesper's fumes aspire;
  And, glimmering to eclipse,
    The long laburnum drips
Its honey of wild flame, its jocund spilth of fire.

Now pass your ways, fair bird, and pass your ways,
*   If you will;*
* I have you through the days!*
* And flit or hold you still,*
* And perch you where you list*
*   On what wrist,—*
* You are mine through the times!*
I have caught you fast for ever in a tangle of sweet rhymes.
*   And in your young maiden morn*
*   You may scorn,*
*   But you must be*

    Bound and sociate to me;
With this thread from out the tomb my dead hand shall
    tether thee?

———

Go, Sister-songs, to that sweet Sister-pair
For whom I have your frail limbs fashionèd,
    And framèd feateously;—
For whom I have your frail limbs fashionèd
With how great shamefastness and how great **dread,**
Knowing you frail, but not if you be fair,
    Though framèd feateously;
    Go unto them from me.
Go from my shadow to their sunshine sight,
    Made for all sights' delight;
Go like twin swans that oar the surgy storms
To bate with pennoned snows in candent air:
    Nigh with abasèd head,
Yourselves linked sisterly, that Sister-pair,
    And go in presence there;
Saying—'Your young eyes cannot see our **forms,**
Nor read the yearning of our looks aright;
But Time shall trail the veilings form our **hair,**
And cleanse your seeing with his euphrasy
(Yea, even your bright seeing make more **bright,**
    Which is all sights' delight),
And ye shall know us for what things we **be.**

'Whilom, within a poet's calyxed heart,
A dewy love we trembled all apart;
    Whence it took rise
    Beneath your radiant eyes,

Which misted it to music. We must long,
A floating haze of silver subtile song,
      Await love-laden
      Above each maiden
The appointed hour that o'er the hearts of you—
      As vapours into dew
      Unweave, whence they were wove,—
Shall turn our loosening musics back to love.'

INSCRIPTION

WHEN the last stir of bubbling melodies
Broke, as my chants sank underneath the wave
Of dulcitude, but sank again to rise
Where man's embaying mind those waters lave
(For music hath its Oceanides
Flexuously floating through their parent seas,
      And such are these),
I saw a vision—or may it be
The effluence of a dear desired reality?
   I saw two spirits high,—
Two spirits, dim within the silver smoke
      Which is for ever woke
By snowing lights of fountained Poesy.
Two shapes they were, familiar as love;
      They were those souls, whereof
One twines from finest gracious daily things,
Strong, constant, noticeless, as are heart-strings,
The golden cage wherein this song-bird sings;
And the other's sun gives hue to all my flowers,
Which else pale flowers of Tartarus would grow,
Where ghosts watch ghosts of blooms in ghostly bowers;—

For we do know
The hidden player by his harmonies,
And by my thoughts I know what still hands thrill the keys.

And to these twain—as from the mind's abysses
All thoughts draw toward the awakening heart's sweet kisses,
With proffer of their wreathen fantasies,—
    Even so to these
I saw how many brought their garlands fair,
Whether of song, or simple love, they were,—
Of simple love, that makes best garlands fair.
But one I marked who lingered still behind,
As for such souls no seemly gift had he:
    He was not of their strain,
Nor worthy of so bright beings to entertain,
Nor fit compeer for such high company.
Yet was he, surely, born to them in mind,
Their youngest nursling of the spirit's kind.
    Last stole this one,
With timid glance, of watching eyes adread,
And dropped his frightened flower when all were gone;
And where the frail flower fell, it witherèd.
But yet methought those high souls smiled thereon;
As when a child, upstraining at your knees
Some fond and fancied nothings, says, 'I give you these!'

LOVE IN DIAN'S LAP

PROEMION

Hear, my Muses, I demand
A little labour at your hand,
 Ere quite is loosed our amity:
A little husband out the sand
 That times the gasps of Poesy!

O belovèd, O ye Two,
When the Years last met, to you
 I sent a gift exultingly.
My song's sands, like the Year's, are few;
 But take this last weak gift from me.

One year ago (one year, one year!)
I had no prescience, no, nor fear;
 I said to Oblivion: 'Dread thou me!'
What cared I for the mortal year?
 I was not of its company.

Before mine own Elect stood I,
And said to Death: 'Not these shall die!'
 I issued mandate royally.
I bade Decay: 'Avoid and fly,
 For I am fatal unto thee.'

I sprinkled a few drops of verse,
And said to Ruin: 'Quit thy hearse;'
    To my Loved: 'Pale not, come with me;
I will escort thee down the years,
    With me thou walk'st immortally.'

Rhyme did I as a charmed cup give,
That who I would might drink and live.
    'Enter,' I cried, 'Song's ark with me!'
And knew not that a witch's sieve
    Were built somewhat more seamanly.

I said unto my heart: 'Be light!
Thy grain will soon for long delight
    Oppress the future's granary:'
Poor fool! and did not hear—'This night
    They shall demand thy song of thee.'

Of God and you I pardon crave;
Who would save others, nor can save
    My own self from mortality:
I throw my whole songs in the grave—
    They will not fill that pit for me.

But thou, to whom I sing this last—
The bitterest bitterness I taste
    Is that thy children have from me
The best I had where all is waste,
    And but the crumbs were cast to thee.

It may be I did little wrong;
Since no notes of thy lyre belong
  To them; thou leftest them for me;
And what didst *thou* want of my song,—
  Thou, thine own immortality?

Ah, I would that I had yet
Given thy head one coronet
  With thine ivies to agree!
Ere thou restest where are set
  Wreaths but on the breast of thee.

Though what avails?—The ivies twined
By thine own hand thou must unbind,
  When there thy temples laid shall be:
'Tis haply Death's prevision kind
  That ungirt brows lie easily.

'Of all thy trees thou lovest so,
None with thee to grave shall go,
  Save the abhorrèd cypress tree.'
The abhorrèd?—Ah, I know, I know,
  Thy dearest follower it would be!

Thou would'st sweetly lie in death
The dark southerner beneath:
  We should interpret, knowing thee,—
'Here I rest' (her symbol saith),
  'And above me, Italy.'

* The words of Horace.

But above thy English grave
Who knows if a tree shall wave?
    Save—when the far certainty
Of thy fame fulfilled is—save
    The laurel that shall spring from thee.

Very little carest thou
If the world no laurel-bough
    Set in thy dead hand, ah me!
But *my* heart to grieve allow
    For the fame thou shalt not see!

Yet my heart to grieve allow,
With the grief that grieves it now,
    Looking to futurity,
With too sure presaging how
    Fools will blind blind eyes from thee:—

Bitterly presaging how
Sightless death must them endow
    With sight, who gladder blind would be.
'Though our eyes be blind enow,
    Let us hide them, lest we see!'

I would their hearts but hardened were
In the way that I aver
    All men shall find this heart of me:
Which is so hard, thy name cut there
    Never worn or blurred can be.

If my song as much might say!
But in all too late a day
    I use thy name for melody;
And with the sweet theme assay
    To hide my descant's poverty.

When that last song gave I you,
Ye and I, beloved Two,
    Were each to each half mystery!
Now the tender veil is through;
    Unafraid the whole we see.

Small for you the danger was!
Statued deity but thaws
    In you to warm divinity;
Some fair defect completion flaws
    With a completing grace to me.

But when *I* my veiling raised—
The Milonian less were crazed
    To talk with men incarnately:
The poor goddess but appraised
    By her lacking arms would be.

Though Pan may have delicious throat,
'Tis hard to tolerate the goat.
    What if Pan were suddenly
To lose his singing, every note?—
    Then pity have of Pan, and me!

Love and Song together sing;
Song is weak and fain to cling
     About Love's shoulder wearily.
Let her voice, poor fainting thing,
     In his strong voice drownèd be!

In my soul's Temple seems a sound
Of unfolding wings around
     The vacant shrine of poesy:
Voices of parting songs resound:—
     'Let us go hence!' *A space let be!*

A space, my Muses,—I demand
This last of labours at your hand,
     Ere quite is loosed our amity:
A little stay the cruel sand
     That times the gasps of Poesy!

BEFORE HER PORTRAIT IN YOUTH

As lovers, banished from their lady's face,
     And hopeless of her grace,
Fashion a ghostly sweetness in its place,
     Fondly adore
Some stealth-won cast attire she wore,
     A kerchief, or a glove:
     And at the lover's beck
Into the glove there fleets a hand,
     Or at impetuous command
Up from the kerchief floats a virgin neck:
So I, in very lowlihead of love,—
     Too shyly reverencing

To let one thought's light footfall smooth
Tread near the living, consecrated thing,—
    Treasure me thy cast youth.
This outworn vesture, tenantless of thee,
        Hath yet my knee,
    For that, with show and semblance fair
        Of the past Her
Who once the beautiful, discarded raimant bare,
        It cheateth me.
    As gale to gale drifts breath
    Of blossoms' death,
So, dropping down the years from hour to hour,
        This dead youth's scent is wafted to me to-day:
I sit, and from the fragrance dream the flower.
        So, then, she looked (I say);
        And so her front sank down
Heavy beneath the poet's iron crown:
        On her mouth museful sweet
        (Even as the twin lips meet)
        Did thought and sadness greet:
            Sighs
        In those mournful eyes
    So put on visibilities;
As viewless ether turns, in deep on deep, to dyes.
        Thus, long ago,
She kept her meditative paces slow
Through maiden meads, with wavèd shadow and gleam
Of locks half-lifted on the winds of dream,
Till Love up-caught her to his chariot's glow.
Yet, voluntary, happier Proserpine!
    This drooping flower of youth thou lettest fall
    I, faring in the cockshut-light, astray,
        Find on my 'lated way,

And stoop, and gather for memorial,
And lay it on my bosom, and make it mine.
To this, the all of love the stars allow me,
   I dedicate and vow me.
   I reach back through the days
A trothed hand to the dead the last trump shall not raise.
   The water-wraith that cries
From those eternal sorrows of thy pictured eyes
Entwines and draws me down their soundless intricacies.

TO A POET BREAKING SILENCE

Too wearily had we and song
Been left to look and left to long,
Yea, song and we to long and look,
Since thine acquainted feet forsook
The mountain where the Muses hymn
For Sinai and the Seraphim.
Now in both the mountains' shine
Dress thy countenance, twice divine!
From Moses and the Muses draw
The Tables of thy double Law!
His rod-born fount and Castaly
Let the one rock bring forth for thee,
Renewing so from either spring
The songs which both thy countries sing:
Or we shall fear lest, heavened thus long,
Thou should'st forget thy native song,
And mar thy mortal melodies
With broken stammer of the skies.

Ah! let the sweet birds of the Lord
With earth's waters make accord;
Teach how the crucifix may be
Carven from the laurel-tree,
Fruit of the Hesperides
Burnish take on Eden-trees,
The Muses' sacred grove be wet
With the red dew of Olivet,
And Sappho lay her burning brows
In white Cecilia's lap of snows!

Thy childhood must have felt the stings
Of too divine o'ershadowings;
Its odorous heart have been a blossom
That in darkness did unbosom,
Those fire-flies of God to invite,
Burning spirits, which by night
Bear upon their laden wing
To such hearts impregnating.
For flowers that night-wings fertilize
Mock down the stars' unsteady eyes,
And with a happy, sleepless glance
Gaze the moon out of countenance.
I think thy girlhood's watchers must
Have took thy folded songs on trust,
And felt them, as one feels the stir
Of still lightnings in the hair,
When conscious hush expects the cloud
To speak the golden secret loud
Which tacit air is privy to;
Flasked in the grape the wine they knew,
Ere thy poet-mouth was able
For its first young starry babble.

Keep'st thou not yet that subtle grace?
Yea, in this silent interspace,
God sets His poems in thy face!

The loom which mortal verse affords,
Out of weak and mortal words,
Wovest thou thy singing-weed in,
To a rune of thy far Eden.
Vain are all disguises! Ah,
Heavenly *incognita!*
Thy mien bewrayeth through that wrong
The great Uranian House of Song!
As the vintages of earth
Taste of the sun that riped their birth,
We know what never-cadent Sun
Thy lampèd clusters throbbed upon,
What plumèd feet the winepress trod;
Thy wine is flavorous of God.
Whatever singing-robe thou wear
Has the Paradisal air;
And some gold feather it has kept
Shows what Floor it lately swept!

"MANUS ANIMAM PINXIT"

LADY who hold'st on me dominion!
Within your spirit's arms I stay me fast
      Against the fell
Immitigate ravening of the gates of hell;
And claiming my right in you, most hardly won,
Of chaste fidelity upon the chaste:
Hold me and hold by me, lest both should fall

(O in high escalade high companion!)
Even in the breach of Heaven's assaulted wall.
Like to a wind-sown sapling grow I from
The clift, Sweet, of your skyward-jetting soul,—
Shook by all gusts that sweep it, overcome
By all its clouds incumbent: O be true
To your soul, dearest, as my life to you!
For if that soil grow sterile, then the whole
Of me must shrivel, from the topmost shoot
Of climbing posey, and my life, killed through,
Dry down and perish to the foodless root.

Sweet Summer! unto you this swallow drew,
  By secret instincts inappeasable,
        That did direct him well,
Lured from his gelid North which wrought him wrong,
        Wintered of sunning song;—
By happy instincts inappeasable,
        Ah yes! that led him well,
Lured to the untried regions and the new
        Climes of auspicious you;
To twitter there, and in his singing dwell.
    But ah! if you, my Summer, should grow waste,
      With grieving skies o'ercast,
For such migration my poor wing was strong
But once; it has no power to fare again
      Forth o'er the heads of men,
Nor other Summers for its Sanctuary:
      But from your mind's chilled sky
It needs must drop, and lie with stiffened wings
      Among your soul's forlornest things;
A speck upon your memory, alack!
A dead fly in a dusty window-crack.

O therefore you who are
What words, being to such mysteries
As raiment to the body is,
Should rather hide than tell;
Chaste and intelligential love:
Whose form is as a grove
Hushed with the cooing of an unseen dove;
Whose spirit to my touch thrills purer far
Than is the tingling of a silver bell;
Whose body other ladies well might bear
As soul,—yea, which it profanation were
For all but you to take as fleshly woof,
Being spirit truest proof;
Whose spirit sure is lineal to that
Which sang *Magnificat:*
Chastest, since such you are,
Take this curbed spirit of mine,
Which your own eyes invest with light divine,
For lofty love and high auxiliar
In daily exalt emprise
Which outsoars mortal eyes;
This soul which on your soul is laid,
As maid's breast against breast of maid;
Beholding how your own I have engraved
On it, and with what purging thoughts have laved
This love of mine from all mortality.
Indeed the copy is a painful one,
And with long labour done!
O if you doubt the thing you are, lady,
Come then, and look in me;
Your beauty, Dian, dress and contemplate
Within a pool to Dian consecrate!

Unveil this spirit, lady, when you will,
For unto all but you 'tis veilèd still:
Unveil, and fearless gaze there, you alone,
And if you love the image—'tis your own!

A CARRIER SONG

I

SINCE you have waned from us,
    Fairest of women!
I am a darkened cage
    Songs cannot hymn in.
My songs have followed you,
    Like birds the summer;
Ah! bring them back to me,
    Swiftly, dear comer!
        Seraphim,
        Her to hymn,
        Might leave their portals;
        And at my feet learn
        The harping of mortals!

II

Where wings to rustle use,
    But this poor tarrier—
Searching my spirit's eaves—
    Find I for carrier.
Ah! bring them back to me
    Swiftly, sweet comer—
Swift, swift, and bring with you
    Song's Indian summer!

Seraphim,
Her to hymn,
Might leave their portals;
And at my feet learn
The harping of mortals!

III

Whereso your angel is,
  My angel goeth;
I am left guardianless,
  Paradise knoweth!
I have no Heaven left
  To weep my wrongs to;
Heaven, when you went from **us,**
  Went with my songs too.
    Seraphim,
    Her to hymn,
    Might leave their portals;
    And at my feet learn
    The harping of mortals!

IV

I have no angels left
  Now, Sweet, to pray to:
Where you have made your **shrine**
  They are away to.
They have struck Heaven's tent,
  And gone to cover you:
Whereso you keep your state
  Heaven is pitched over you!

> *Seraphim,*
> *Her to hymn,*
> *Might leave their portals;*
> *And at my feet learn*
> *The harping of mortals!*

V

She that is Heaven's Queen
   Her title borrows,
For that she, pitiful,
   Beareth our sorrows.
So thou, *Regina mî,*
   Spes infirmorum;
With all our grieving crowned
   Mater dolorum!
> *Seraphim,*
> *Her to hymn,*
> *Might leave their portals;*
> *And at my feet learn*
> *The harping of mortals!*

VI

Yet, envious coveter
   Of others' grieving!
This lonely longing yet
   'Scapeth your reaving.
Cruel, to take from a
   Sinner his Heaven!
Think you with contrite smiles
   To be forgiven?

> *Seraphim,*
> *Her to hymn,*
> *Might leave their portals;*
> *And at my feet learn*
> *The harping of mortals!*

VII

Penitent! give me back
  Angels, and Heaven;
Render your stolen self,
  And be forgiven!
How frontier Heaven from you?
  For my soul prays, Sweet,
Still to your face in Heaven,
  Heaven in your face. Sweet!
> *Seraphim,*
> *Her to hymn,*
> *Might leave their portals;*
> *And at my feet learn*
> *The harping of mortals!*

SCALA JACOBI PORTAQUE EBURNEA

HER soul from earth to Heaven lies,
Like the ladder of the vision,
    Whereon go
    To and fro,
In ascension and demission,
Star-flecked feet of Paradise.

Now she is drawn up from me,
All my angels, wet-eyed, tristful,
    Gaze from great
    Heaven's gate
Like pent children, very wistful,
That below a playmate see.

Dream-dispensing face of hers!
Ivory port which loosed upon me
    Wings, I wist,
    Whose amethyst
Trepidations have forgone me,—
Hesper's filmy traffickers!

GILDED GOLD

THOU dost to rich attire a grace,
To let it deck itself with thee,
And teachest pomp strange cunning ways
To be thought simplicity.
But lilies, stolen from grassy mold,
No more curlèd state unfold
Translated to a vase of gold;
In burning throne though they keep still
Serenities unthawed and chill.
Therefore, albeit thou'rt stately so,
In statelier state thou us'dst to go.

Though jewels should phosphoric burn
Through those night-waters of thine hair,
A flower from its translucid urn
Poured silver flame more lunar-fair.

These futile trappings but recall
Degenerate worshippers who fall
In purfled kirtle and brocade
To 'parel the white Mother-Maid.
For, as her image stood arrayed
In vests of its self-substance wrought
To measure of the sculptor's thought—
Slurred by those added braveries;
So for thy spirit did devise
Its Maker seemly garniture,
Of its own essence parcel pure,—
From grave simplicities a dress,
And reticent demurenesses,
And love encinctured with reserve;
Which the woven vesture should subserve.
For outward robes in their ostents
Should show the soul's habiliments.
Therefore I say,—Thou'rt fair even so,
But better Fair I used to know.

The violet would thy dusk hair deck
With graces like thine own unsought.
Ah! but such place would daze and wreck
Its simple, lowly, rustic thought;
For so advancèd, dear, to thee,
It would unlearn humility!
Yet do not, with an altered look,
In these weak numbers read rebuke;
Which are but jealous lest too much
God's master-piece thou shouldst retouch.
Where a sweetness is complete,
Add not sweets unto the sweet!
Or, as thou wilt, for others so

In unfamiliar richness go;
But keep for mine acquainted eyes
The fashions of thy Paradise.

HER PORTRAIT

OH, but the heavenly grammar did I hold
Of that high speech which angels' tongues turn gold!
So should her deathless beauty take no wrong,
Praised in her own great kindred's fit and cognate tongue:
Or if that language yet with us abode
Which Adam in the garden talked with God!
But our untempered speech descends—poor heirs!
Grimy and rough-cast still from Babel's bricklayers:
Curse on the brutish jargon we inherit,
Strong but to damn, not memorize, a spirit!
A cheek, a lip, a limb, a bosom, they
Move with light ease in speech of working-day;
And women we do use to praise even so.
But here the gates we burst, and to the temple go.
Their praise were her dispraise: who dare, who dare,
Adulate the seraphim for their burning hair?
How, if with them I dared, here should I dare it?
How praise the woman, who but know the spirit?
How praise the colour of her eyes, uncaught
While they were coloured with her varying thought?
How her mouth's shape, who only use to know
What tender shape her speech will fit it to?
Or her lips' redness, when their joinèd veil
Song's fervid hand has parted till it wore them pale?

If I would praise her soul (temerarious if!),
All must be mystery and hieroglyph.
Heaven, which not oft is prodigal of its more
To singers, in their song too great before
(By which the hierarch of large poesy is
Restrained to his one sacred benefice),
Only for her the salutary awe
Relaxes and stern canon of its law;
To her alone concedes pluralities,
In her alone to reconcile agrees
The Muse, the Graces, and the Charities;
To her, who can the trust so well conduct,
To her it gives the use, to us the usufruct.

What of the dear administress then may
I utter, though I spoke her own carved perfect way?
What of her daily gracious converse known,
Whose heavenly despotism must needs dethrone
And subjugate all sweetness but its own?
Deep in my heart subsides the infrequent word,
And there dies slowly throbbing like a wounded bird.
What of her silence, that outsweetens speech?
What of her thoughts, high marks for mine own thoughts
    to reach?
Yet, (Chaucer's antique sentence so to turn)
Most gladly will she teach, and gladly learn;
And teaching her, by her enchanting art,
The master threefold learns for all he can impart.
Now all is said, and all being said,—aye me!
There yet remains unsaid the very She.
Nay, to conclude (so to conclude I dare),
If of her virtues you evade the snare,
Then for her faults you'll fall in love with her.

Alas, and I have spoken of her Muse—
Her Muse, that died with her auroral dews!
Learn, the wise cherubim from harps of gold
Seduce a trepidating music manifold;
But the superior seraphim do know
None other music but to flame and glow.
So she first lighted on our frosty earth,
A sad musician, of cherubic birth,
Playing to alien ears—which did not prize
The uncomprehended music of the skies—
The exiled airs of her far Paradise.
But soon, from her own harpings taking fire,
In love and light her melodies expire.
Now Heaven affords her, for her silenced hymn,
A double portion of the seraphim.

At the rich odours from her heart that rise,
My soul remembers its lost Paradise,
And antenatal gales blow from Heaven's shores of spice;
I grow essential all, uncloaking me
From this encumbering virility,
And feel the primal sex of heaven and poetry:
And, parting from her, in me linger on
Vague snatches of Uranian antiphon.

How to the petty prison could she shrink
Of femineity?—Nay, but I think
In a dear courtesy her spirit would
Woman assume, for grace to womanhood.
Or, votaress to the virgin Sanctitude
Of reticent withdrawal's sweet, courted pale,
She took the cloistral flesh, the sexual veil,
Of her sad, aboriginal sisterhood;
The habit of cloistral flesh which founding Eve indued.

Thus do I know her. But for what men call
Beauty—the loveliness corporeal,
Its most just praise a thing unproper were
To singer or to listener, me or her.
She wears that body but as one indues;
A robe, half careless, for it is the use;
Although her soul and it so fair agree,
We sure may, unattaint of heresy,
Conceit it might the soul's begetter be.
The immortal could we cease to contemplate,
The mortal part suggests its every trait.
God laid His fingers on the ivories
Of her pure members as on smoothèd keys,
And there out-breathed her spirit's harmonies.
I'll speak a little proudly:—I disdain
To count the beauty worth my wish or gain,
Which the dull daily fool can covet or obtain.
I do confess the fairness of the spoil,
But from such rivalry it takes a soil.
For her I'll proudlier speak:—how could it be
That I should praise the gilding on the psaltery?
'Tis not for her to hold that prize a prize,
Or praise much praise, though proudest in its wise,
To which even hopes of merely women rise.
Such strife would to the vanquished laurels yield,
Against *her* suffered to have lost a field.
Herself must with herself be sole compeer,
Unless the people of her distant sphere
Some gold migration send to melodize the year.
But first our hearts must burn in larger guise,
To reformate the uncharitable skies,
And so the deathless plumage to acclimatize:
Since this, their sole congener in our clime,
Droops her sad, ruffled thoughts for half the shivering time.

Yet I have felt what terrors may consort
In women's cheeks, the Graces' soft resort;
My hand hath shook at gentle hands' access,
And trembled at the waving of a tress;
My blood known panic fear, and fled dismayed,
Where ladies' eyes have set their ambuscade;
The rustle of a robe hath been to me
The very rattle of love's musketry;
Although my heart hath beat the loud advance,
I have recoiled before a challenging glance,
Proved gay alarms where warlike ribbons dance.
And from it all, this knowledge have I got,—
The whole that others have, is less than they have not;
All which makes other women noted fair,
Unnoted would remain and overshone in her.

How should I gauge what beauty is her dole,
Who cannot see her countenance for her soul,
As birds see not the casement for the sky?
And, as 'tis check they prove its presence by,
I know not of her body till I find
My flight debarred the heaven of her mind.
Hers is the face whence all should copied be,
Did God make replicas of such as she;
Its presence felt by what it does abate,
Because the soul shines through tempered and mitigate:
Where—as a figure labouring at night
Beside the body of a splendid light—
Dark Time works hidden by its luminousness;
And every line he labours to impress
Turns added beauty, like the veins that run
Athwart a leaf which hangs against the sun.

There regent Melancholy wide controls;
There Earth- and Heaven-Love play for aureoles;
There Sweetness out of Sadness breaks at fits,
Like bubbles on dark water, or as flits
A sudden silver fin through its deep infinites;
There amorous Thought has sucked pale Fancy's breath,
And Tenderness sits looking toward the lands of Death:
There Feeling stills her breathing with her hand,
And Dream from Melancholy part wrests the wand;
And on this lady's heart, looked you so deep,
Poor Poetry has rocked himself to sleep:
Upon the heavy blossom of her lips
Hangs the bee Musing; nigh her lids eclipse
Each half-occulted star beneath that lies;
And, in the contemplation of those eyes,
Passionless passion, wild tranquillities.

EPILOGUE TO THE POET'S SITTER

Wherein he excuseth himself for the manner of the Portrait.

ALAS! now wilt thou chide, and say (I deem)
My figure descant hides the simple theme:
Or, in another wise reproving, say
I ill observe thine own high reticent way.
Oh, pardon, that I testify of thee
What thou couldst never speak, nor others be!

Yet (for the book is not more innocent
Of what the gazer's eyes make so intent),
She will but smile, perhaps, that I find my fair
Sufficing scope in such a strait theme as her.

'Bird of the sun! the stars' wild honey-bee!
Is your gold browsing done so thoroughly?
Or sinks a singèd wing to narrow nest in me?'
(Thus she might say: for not this lowly vein
Out-deprecates her deprecating strain.)
Oh, you mistake, dear lady, quite; nor know
Ether was strict as you, its loftiness as low!

The heavens do not advance their majesty
Over their marge; beyond his empery
The ensigns of the wind are not unfurled,
His reign is hooped in by the pale o' the world.
'Tis not the continent, but the contained,
That pleasaunce makes or prison, loose or chained.
Too much alike or little captives me,
For all oppression is captivity.

What groweth to its height demands no higher;
The limit limits not, but the desire.
Our minds make their own Termini, nor call
The issuing circumscriptions great or small;
So high constructing Nature lessons to us all:
Who optics gives accommodate to see
Your countenance large as looks the sun to be,
And distant greatness less than near humanity.

We, therefore, with a sure instinctive mind,
An equal spaciousness of bondage find
In confines far or near, of air or our own kind.
Our looks and longings, which affronts the stars,
Most richly bruised against their golden bars,
Delighted captives of their flaming spears,
Find a restraint restrainless which appears

As that is, and so simply natural,
In you;—the fair detention freedom call,
And overscroll with fancies the loved prison-wall.

Such sweet captivity, and only such,
In you, as in those golden bars, we touch!
Our gazes for sufficing limits know
The firmament above, your face below;
Our longings are contented with the skies,
Contented with the heaven, and your eyes.
My restless wings, that beat the whole world through,
Flag on the confines of the sun and you;
And find the human pale remoter of the two.

DOMUS TUA

A PERFECT woman—Thine be laud!
Her body is a Temple of God.
At Doom-bar dare I make avows:
I have loved the beauty of Thy house.

IN HER PATHS

AND she has trod before me in these ways!
I think that she has left here heavenlier days;
And I do guess her passage, as the skies
        Of holy Paradise
        Turn deeply holier,
And, looking up with sudden new delight,
One knows a seraph-wing has passed in flight.

The air is purer for her breathing, sure!
    And all the fields do wear
    The beauty fallen from her;
The winds do brush me with her robe's allure.
'Tis she has taught the heavens to look sweet,
    And they do but repeat
The heaven, heaven, heaven of her face!
The clouds have studied going from her grace!
The pools whose marges had forgot the tread
Of Naiad, disenchanted, fled,
      A second time must mourn,
      Bereaven and forlorn.

Ah, foolish pools and meads! You did not see
Essence of old, essential pure as she.
For this was even that Lady, and none other,
The man in me calls 'Love,' the child calls 'Mother.'

AFTER HER GOING

    THE after-even! Ah, did I walk,
      Indeed, in her or even?
    For nothing of me or around
      But absent She did leaven,
    Felt in my body as its soul,
      And in my soul its heaven.

    'Ah me! my very flesh turns soul,
      Essenced,' I sighed, 'with bliss!'
    And the blackbird held his lutany,
      All fragrant-through with bliss;
    And all things stilled were as a maid
      Sweet with a single kiss.

For grief of perfect fairness, eve
    Could nothing do but smile;
The time was far too perfect fair,
    Being but for a while;
And ah, in me, too happy grief
    Blinded herself with smile!

The sunset at its radiant heart
    Had somewhat unconfest:
The bird was loath of speech, its song
    Half-refluent on its breast,
And made melodious toyings with
    A note or two at best.

And she was gone, my sole, my Fair,
    Ah, sole my Fair, was gone!
Methinks, throughout the world 'twere right
    I had been sad alone;
And yet, such sweet in all things' heart,
    And such sweet in my own!

BENEATH A PHOTOGRAPH

PHŒBUS, who taught me art divine,
Here tried his hand where I did mine;
And his white fingers in this face
Set my Fair's sigh-suggesting grace.
O sweetness past profaning guess,
Grievous with its own exquisiteness!
Vesper-like face, its shadows bright
With meanings of sequestered light;
Drooped with shamefast sanctities

She purely fears eyes cannot miss,
Yet would blush to know she *is*.
Ah, who can view with passionless glance
This tear-compelling countenance?
He has cozened it to tell
Almost its own miracle.
Yet I, all-viewing though he be,
Methinks saw further here than he;
And, Master gay, I swear I drew
Something the better of the two!

THE HOUND OF HEAVEN

I FLED Him, down the nights and down the days;
  I fled Him, down the arches of the years;
I fled Him, down the labyrinthine ways
  Of my own mind; and in the mist of tears
I hid from Him, and under running laughter.
      Up vistaed hopes I sped;
      And shot, precipitated,
Adown Titanic glooms of chasmèd fears,
  From those strong Feet that followed, followed after.
      But with unhurrying chase,
      And unperturbèd pace,
  Deliberate speed, majestic instancy,
      They beat—and a Voice beat
      More instant than the Feet—
  'All things betray thee, who betrayest Me.'

      I pleaded, outlaw-wise,
By many a hearted casement, curtained red,
  Trellised with intertwining charities;
(For, though I knew His love Who followèd,
      Yet was I sore adread
Lest, having Him, I must have naught beside.)
But, if one little casement parted wide,
  The gust of His approach would clash it to:
  Fear wist not to evade, as Love wist to pursue.
Across the margent of the world I fled,

88

And troubled the gold gateways of the stars,
  Smiting for shelter on their clangèd bars;
      Fretted to dulcet jars
And silvern chatter the pale ports o' the moon.
I said to Dawn: Be sudden—to Eve: Be soon;
  With thy young skiey blossoms heap me over
      From this tremendous Lover—
Float thy vague veil about me, lest He see!
  I tempted all His servitors, but to find
My own betrayal in their constancy,
In faith to Him their fickleness to me,
  Their traitorous trueness, and their loyal deceit.
To all swift things for swiftness did I sue;
  Clung to the whistling mane of every wind.
    But whether they swept, smoothly fleet,
    The long savannahs of the blue;
      Or whether, Thunder-driven,
      They clanged his chariot 'thwart a heaven,
Plashy with flying lightnings round the spurn o' their feet:—
  Fear wist not to evade as Love wist to pursue.
      Still with unhurrying chase,
      And unperturbèd pace,
    Deliberate speed, majestic instancy,
      Came on the following Feet,
      And a Voice above their beat—
'Naught shelters thee, who wilt not shelter Me.'

I sought no more that after which I strayed
      In face or man or maid;
But still within the little children's eyes
    Seems something, something that replies,
They at least are for me, surely for me!
I turned me to them very wistfully;

But just as their young eyes grew sudden fair
    With dawning answers there,
Their angel plucked them from me by the hair.
'Come then, ye other children, Nature's—share
With me' (said I) 'your delicate fellowship;
    Let me greet you lip to lip,
    Let me twine with you caresses,
      Wantoning
    With our Lady-Mother's vagrant tresses,
      Banqueting
    With her in her wind-walled palace,
    Underneath her azured daïs,
    Quaffing, as your taintless way is,
      From a chalice
Lucent-weeping out of the dayspring.'
    So it was done:
I in their delicate fellowship was one—
Drew the bolt of Nature's secrecies.
    I knew all the swift importings
    On the wilful face of skies;
    I knew how the clouds arise
    Spumèd of the wild sea-snortings;
      All that's born or dies
    Rose and drooped with; made them shapers
Of mine own moods, or wailful or divine;
    With them joyed and was bereaven.
    I was heavy with the even,
    When she lit her glimmering tapers
    Round the day's dead sanctities.
    I laughed in the morning's eyes.
I triumphed and I saddened with all weather,
    Heaven and I wept together,
And its sweet tears were salt with mortal mine;

Against the red throb of its sunset-heart
    I laid my own to beat,
    And share commingling heat;
But not by that, by that, was eased my human smart.
In vain my tears were wet on Heaven's grey cheek.
For ah! we know not what each other says,
    These things and I; in sound *I* speak—
Their sound is but their stir, they speak by silences.
Nature, poor stepdame, cannot slake my drouth;
    Let her, if she would owe me,
Drop yon blue bosom-veil of sky, and show me
    The breasts o' her tenderness:
Never did any milk of hers once bless
      My thirsting mouth.
      Nigh and nigh draws the chase.
      With unperturbèd pace,
    Deliberate speed, majestic instancy;
      And past those noisèd Feet
      A voice comes yet more fleet—
    'Lo! naught contents thee, who content'st not Me.'

Naked I wait Thy love's uplifted stroke!
My harness piece by piece Thou hast hewn from me,
    And smitten me to my knee;
    I am defenceless utterly.
    I slept, methinks, and woke,
And, slowly gazing, find me stripped in sleep.
In the rash lustihead of my young powers,
    I shook the pillaring hours
And pulled my life upon me; grimed with smears,
I stand amid the dust o' the mounded years—
My mangled youth lies dead beneath the heap.
My days have crackled and gone up in smoke,

Have puffed and burst as sun-starts on a stream.
      Yea, faileth now even dream
The dreamer, and the lute the lutanist;
Even the linked fantasies, in whose blossomy twist
I swung the earth a trinket at my wrist,
Are yielding; cords of all too weak account
For earth with heavy griefs so overplussed.
      Ah! is Thy love indeed
A weed, albeit an amaranthine weed,
Suffering no flowers except its own to mount?
      Ah! must—
      Designer infinite!—
Ah! must Thou char the wood ere Thou canst limn with it?
My freshness spent its wavering shower i' the dust;
And now my heart is as a broken fount,
Wherein tear-drippings stagnate, spilt down ever
      From the dank thoughts that shiver
Upon the sighful branches of my mind.
      Such is; what is to be?
The pulp so bitter, how shall taste the rind?
I dimly guess what Time in mists confounds;
Yet ever and anon a trumpet sounds
From the hid battlements of Eternity;
Those shaken mists a space unsettle, then
Round the half-glimpsèd turrets slowly wash again.
      But not ere him who summoneth
      I first have seen, enwound
With glooming robes purpureal, cypress-crowned;
His name I know, and what his trumpet saith.
Whether man's heart or life it be which yields
      Thee harvest, must Thy harvest-fields
      Be dunged with rotten death?

Now of that long pursuit
Comes on at hand the bruit;
That Voice is round me like a bursting sea:
      'And is thy earth so marred,
      Shattered in shard on shard?
Lo, all things fly thee, for thou fliest Me!
Strange, piteous, futile thing!
Wherefore should any set thee love apart?
Seeing none but I makes much of naught' (He said),
'And human love needs human meriting:
      How hast thou merited—
Of all man's clotted clay the dingiest clot?
      Alack, thou knowest not
How little worthy of any love thou art!
Whom wilt thou find to love ignoble thee,
      Save Me, save only Me?
All which I took from thee I did but take,
      Not for thy harms,
But just that thou might'st seek it in My arms.
      All which thy child's mistake
Fancies as lost, I have stored for thee at home:
      Rise, clasp My hand, and come!'
   Halts by me that footfall:
   Is my gloom, after all,
Shade of His hand, outstretched caressingly?
   'Ah, fondest, blindest, weakest,
   I am He Whom thou seekest!
Thou dravest love from thee, who dravest Me.'

ODE TO THE SETTING SUN

PRELUDE

The wailful sweetness of the violin
  Floats down the hushèd waters of the wind,
The heart-strings of the throbbing harp begin
  To long in aching music. Spirit-pined,

In wafts that poignant sweetness drifts, until
  The wounded soul ooze sadness. The red sun,
A bubble of fire, drops slowly toward the hill,
  While one bird prattles that the day is done.

O setting Sun, that as in reverent days
  Sinkest in music to thy smoothèd sleep,
Discrowned of homage, though yet crowned with rays,
  Hymned not at harvest more, though reapers reap:

For thee this music wakes not. O deceived,
  If thou hear in these thoughtless harmonies
A pious phantom of adorings reaved,
  And echo of fair ancient flatteries!

Yet, in this field where the Cross planted reigns,
  I know not what strange passion bows my head
To thee, whose great command upon my veins
  Proves thee a god for me not dead, not dead!

For worship it is too incredulous,
    For doubt—oh, too believing-passionate!
What wild divinity makes my heart thus
    A fount of most baptismal tears?—Thy straight

Long geam lies steady on the Cross. Ah me!
    What secret would thy radiant finger show?
Of thy bright mastership is this the key?
    Is *this* thy secret, then? And is it woe?

Fling from thine ear the burning curls, and hark
    A song thou hast not heard in Northern day;
For Rome too daring, and for Greece too dark,
    Sweet with wild things that pass, that pass away!

ODE

Alpha and Omega, sadness and mirth,
    The springing music, and its wasting breath—
The fairest things in life are Death and Birth,
    And of these two the fairer thing is Death.
Mystical twins of Time inseparable,
    The younger hath the holier array,
        And hath the awfuller sway:
It is the falling star that trails the light,
It is the breaking wave that hath the might,
The passing shower that rainbows maniple.
    Is it not so, O thou down-striken Day,
That draw'st thy splendours round thee in thy fall?
High was thine Eastern pomp inaugural;
But thou dost set in statelier pageantry,
    Lauded with tumults of a firmament:

Thy visible music-blasts make deaf the sky,
   Thy cymbals clang to fire the Occident,
Thou dost thy dying so triumphally:
I *see* the crimson blaring of thy shawms!
     Why doth those lucent palms
Strew thy feet's failing thicklier than their might,
Who dost but hood thy glorious eyes with night,
And vex the heels of all the yesterdays?
     Lo! this loud, lackeying praise
Will stay behind to greet the usurping moon,
   When they have cloud-barred over thee the West.
Oh, shake the bright dust from thy parting shoon!
   The earth not pæans thee, nor serves thy hest;
Be godded not by Heaven! avert thy face,
     And leave to blank disgrace
The oblivious world! unsceptre thee of state and place!

Ha! but bethink thee what thou gazedst on,
   Ere yet the snake Decay had venomed tooth;
The name thou bar'st in those vast seasons gone—
     Candid Hyperion,
   Clad in the light of thine immortal youth!
     Ere Dionysus bled thy vines,
Or Artemis drave her clamours through the wood,
    Thou saw'st how once against Olympus' height
     The brawny Titans stood,
And shook the gods' world 'bout their ears, and how
Enceladus (whom Etna cumbers now)
   Shouldered me Pelion with its swinging pines,
The river unrecked, that did its broken flood
Spurt on his back: before the mountainous shock
     The rankèd gods dislock,
Scared to their skies; wide o'er rout-trampled night

Flew spurned the pebbled stars: those splendours **then**
  Had tempested on earth, star upon star
  Mounded in ruin, if a longer war
Had quaked Olympus and cold-fearing men.
      Then did the ample marge
      And circuit of thy targe
  Sullenly redden all the vaward fight,
      Above the blusterous clash
      Wheeled thy swung falchion's flash,
  And hewed their forces into splintered flight.

Yet ere Olympus thou wast, and a god!
      Though we deny thy nod,
We cannot spoil thee of thy divinity.
      What know we elder than thee?
When thou didst, bursting from the great void's **husk,**
Leap like a lion on the throat o' the dusk;
      When the angels rose-chapleted
        Sang each to other,
      The vaulted blaze overhead
      Of their vast pinions spread,
        Hailing thee brother;
How chaos rolled back from the wonder,
And the First Morn knelt down to thy visage of **thunder!**
      Thou didst draw to thy side
      Thy young Auroral bride,
 And lift her veil of night and mystery;
      Tellus with baby hands
      Shook off her swaddling-bands,
 And from the unswathèd vapours laughed to thee.

Thou twi-form deity, nurse at once and sire!
  Thou genitor that all things nourishest!
  The earth was suckled at thy shining breast,
And in her veins is quick thy milky fire.
Who scarfed her with the morning? and who set
Upon her brow the day-fall's carcanet?
    Who queened her front with the enrondured moon?
      Who dug nights' jewels from their vaulty mine
        To dower her, past an eastern wizard's dreams,
    When, hovering on him through his haschish-swoon,
      All the rained gems of the old Tartarian line
Shiver in lustrous throbbings of tinged flame?
        Whereof a moiety in the Paolis' seams
        Statelily builded their Venetian name.
          Thou hast enwoofèd her
          An empress of the air,
And all her births are propertied by thee:
          Her teeming centuries
          Drew being from thine eyes:
Thou fatt'st the marrow of all quality.

Who lit the furnace of the mammoth's heart?
  Who shagged him like Pilatus' ribbèd flanks?
      Who raised the columned ranks
Of that old pre-diluvian forestry,
Which like a continent torn oppressed the sea,
  When the ancient heavens did in rains depart,
      While the high-dancèd whirls
Of the tossed scud made hiss thy drenchèd curls?
      Thou rear'dst the enormous brood;
      Who hast with life imbued
  The lion maned in tawny majesty,

The tiger velvet-barred,
The stealthy-stepping pard,
And the lithe panther's flexous symmetry?

How came the entombèd tree a light-bearer,
    Though sunk in lightless lair?
    Friend of the forgers of earth,
Mate of the earthquake and thunders volcanic,
Clasped in the arms of the forces Titanic
    Which rock like a cradle the girth
      Of the ether-hung world;
Swart son of the swarthy mine,
When flame on the breath of his nostrils feeds
    How is his countenance half-divine,
    Like thee in thy sanguine weeds?
Thou gavest him his light,
Though sepultured in night
Beneath the dead bones of a perished world;
    Over his prostrate form
    Though cold, and heat, and storm,
The mountainous wrack of a creation hurled.

    Who made the splendid rose
    Saturate with purple glows;
Cupped to the marge with beauty; a perfume-press
    Whence the wind vintages
Gushes of warmèd fragrance richer far
Than all the flavorous ooze of Cyprus' vats?
Lo, in yon gale which waves her green cymar,
    With dusky cheeks burnt red
    She sways her heavy head,
Drunk with the must of her own odorousness;
    While in a moted trouble the vexed gnats

Maze, and vibrate, and tease the noontide hush.
　　Who girt dissolvèd lightnings in the grape?
Summered the opal with an Irised flush?
　　　Is it not thou that dost the tulip drape,
　　　　And huest the daffodilly,
　　　　Yet who hast snowed the lily,
And her frail sister, whom the waters name,
　　Dost vestal-vesture 'mid the blaze of June,
　　Cold as the new-sprung girlhood of the moon
Ere Autumn's kiss sultry her cheek with flame?
　　　　Thou sway'st thy sceptred beam
　　　　O'er all delight and dream,
　　Beauty is beautiful but in thy glance:
　　　　And like a jocund maid
　　　　In garland-flowers arrayed,
　　Before thy ark Earth keeps her sacred dance.

And now, O shaken from thine antique throne,
　　And sunken from thy cœrule empery,
Now that the red glare of thy fall is blown
　　In smoke and flame about the windy sky,
Where are the wailing voices that should meet
　　From hill, stream, grove, and all of mortal shape
Who tread thy gifts, in vineyards as stray feet
　　Pulp the globed weight of juiced Iberia's grape?
　　　　Where is the threne o' the sea?
　　　　And why not dirges thee
The wind, that sings to himself as he makes stride
　　Lonely and terrible on the Andèan height?
　　　Where is the Naid 'mid her sworded sedge?
　　The Nymph wan-glimmering by her wan fount's verge?
The Dryad at timid gaze by the wood-side?
　　　　The Oread jutting light

On one up-strainèd sole from the rock-ledge?
   The Nereid tip-toe on the scud o' the surge,
With whistling tresses dank athwart her face,
And all her figure poised in lithe Circean grace?
      Why withers their lament?
      Their tresses tear-besprent,
   Have they sighed hence with trailing garment-hem?
      O sweet, O sad, O fair,
      I catch your flying hair,
   Draw your eyes down to me, and dream on them!

A space, and they fleet from me. Must ye fade—
O old, essential candours, ye who made
   The earth a living and a radiant thing—
      And leave her corpse in our strained, cheated arms?
      Lo ever thus, when Song with chorded charms
Draws from dull death his lost Eurydice,
   Lo ever thus, even at consummating,
   Even in the swooning minute that claims her his,
   Even as he trembles to the impassioned kiss
   Of reincarnate Beauty, his control
   Clasps the cold body, and forgoes the soul!
      Whatso looks lovelily
Is but the rainbow on life's weeping rain.
Why have we longings of immortal pain,
And all we long for mortal? Woe is me,
And all our chants but chaplet some decay,
As mine this vanishing—nay, vanished Day.
The low sky-line dusks to a leaden hue,
   No rift disturbs the heavy shade and chill,
Save one, where the charred firmament lets through
   The scorching dazzle of Heaven; 'gainst which the hill,
      Out-flattened sombrely,

Stands black as life against eternity.
　　　Against eternity?
　　　A rifting light in me
Burns through the leaden broodings of the mind:
　　　O blessèd Sun, thy state
　　　Uprisen or derogate
Dafts me no more with doubt; I seek and find.

　　　If with exultant tread
　　　　Thou foot the Eastern sea,
　　　　Or like a golden bee
　　　Sting the West to angry red,
　　　Thou dost image, thou dost follow
　　　　That King-Maker of Creation,
　　　Who, ere Hellas hailed Apollo,
　　　　Gave thee, angel-god, thy station;
Thou art of Him a type memorial.
　　Like Him thou hang'st in dreadful pomp of blood
　　　　Upon thy Western rood;
　　And His stained brow did vail like thine to night,
　　　　Yet lift once more Its light,
And, risen, again departed from our ball,
But when It set on earth arose in Heaven.
Thus hath He unto death His beauty given:
And so of all which form inheriteth
　　　The fall doth pass the rise in worth;
For birth hath in itself the germ of death,
　　But death hath in itself the germ of birth.
It is the falling acorn buds the tree,
The falling rain that bears the greenery,
　　The fern-plants moulder when the ferns arise.
　　For there is nothing lives but something dies,
And there is nothing dies but something lives.

Till skies be fugitives,
Till Time, the hidden root of change, updries,
Are Birth and Death inseparable on earth;
For they are twain yet one, and Death is Birth.

AFTER-STRAIN

Now with wan ray that other sun of Song
    Sets in the bleakening waters of my soul:
One step, and lo! the Cross stands gaunt and long
    'Twixt me and yet bright skies, a presaged dole.

Even so, O Cross! thine is the victory.
    Thy roots are fast within our fairest fields;
Brightness may emanate in Heaven from thee,
    Here thy dread symbol only shadow yields.

Of reapèd joys thou art the heavy sheaf
    Which must be lifted, though the reaper groan;
Yea, we may cry till Heaven's great ear be deaf,
    But we must bear thee, and must bear alone.

Vain were a Simon; of the Antipodes
    Our night not borrows the superfluous day.
Yet woe to him that from his burden flees,
    Crushed in the fall of what he cast away.

Therefore, O tender Lady, Queen Mary,
    Thou gentleness that dost enmoss and drape
The Cross's rigorous austerity,
    Wipe thou the blood from wounds that needs must gape.

'Lo, though suns rise and set, but crosses stay,
    I leave thee ever,' saith she, 'light of cheer.'
'Tis so: yon sky still thinks upon the Day,
    And showers aërial blossoms on his bier.

Yon cloud with wrinkled fire is edgèd sharp;
    And once more welling through the air, ah me!
How the sweet viol plains him to the harp,
    Whose pangèd sobbings throng tumultuously.

Oh, this Medusa-pleasure with her stings!
    This essence of all suffering, which is joy!
I am not thankless for the spell it brings,
    Though tears must be told down for the charmed toy.

No; while soul, sky, and music bleed together,
    Let me give thanks even for those griefs in me,
The restless windward stirrings of whose feather
    Prove them the brood of immortality.

My soul is quitted of death-neighbouring swoon,
    Who shall not slake her immitigable scars
Until she hear 'My sister!' from the moon,
    And take the kindred kisses of the stars.

TO THE DEAD CARDINAL OF WESTMINSTER

(Henry Edward Manning: Died January 1892)

I WILL not perturbate
Thy Paradisal state
    With praise
  Of thy dead days;

To the new-heavened say,
'Spirit, thou wert fine clay':
    This do,
  Thy praise who knew.

Therefore my spirit clings
Heaven's porter by the wings,
    And holds
  Its gated golds

Apart, with thee to press
A private business:—
    Whence,
  Deign me audience.

Anchorite, who didst dwell
With all the world for cell,
    My soul
  Round me doth roll

A sequestration bare.
Too far alike we were,
    To far
    Dissimilar.

For its burning fruitage I
Do climb the tree o' the sky;
    Do prize
    Some human eyes.

You smelt the Heaven-blossoms,
And all the sweet embosoms
    The dear
    Uranian year.

Those Eyes my weak gaze shuns,
Which to the suns are Suns,
    Did
    Not affray your lid.

The carpet was let down
(With golden moultings strown)
    For you
    Of the angels' blue.

But I, ex-Paradised,
The shoulder of your Christ
    Find high
    To lean thereby.

So flaps my helpless sail,
Bellying with neither gale,
    Of Heaven
    Nor Orcus even.

Life is coquetry
Of death, which wearies me,
    Too sure
    Of the amour;

A tiring-room where I
Death's divers garments try,
    Till fit
    Some fashion sit.

It seemeth me too much
I do rehearse for such
    A mean
    And single scene.

The sandy glass hence bear—
Antique remembrancer:
    My veins
    Do spare its pains.

With secret sympathy
My thoughts repeat in me
    Infirm
    The turn o' the worm

Beneath my appointed sod;
The grave is in my blood;
    I shake
    To winds that take

Its grasses by the top;
The rains thereon that drop
    Perturb
    With drip acerb

My subtly answering soul;
The feet across its knoll
        Do jar
    Me from afar.

As sap foretastes the spring;
As Earth ere blossoming
        Thrills
    With far daffodils,

And feels her breast turn sweet
With the unconceivèd wheat;
        So doth
    My flesh foreloathe

The abhorrèd spring of Dis,
With seething presciences
        Affirm
    The preparate worm.

I have no thought that I,
When at the last I die,
        Shall reach
    To gain your speech.

But you, should that be so,
May very well, I know,
        May well
    To me in hell

With recognizing eyes
Look down from your Paradise—
        'God bless
    Thy hopelessness!'

Call, holy soul, O call
The hosts angelical,
  And say,—
 'See, far away

'Lies one I saw on earth;
One stricken from his birth
  With curse
 Of destinate verse.

'What place doth He ye serve
For such sad spirit reserve,—
  Given,
 In dark lieu of Heaven,

'The impitiable Dæmon,
Beauty, to adore and dream on.
  To be
 Perpetually

'Hers, but she never his?
He reapeth miseries;
  Foreknows
 His wages woes;

'He lives detachèd days;
He serveth not for praise;
  For gold
 He is not sold;

'Deaf is he to world's tongue;
He scorneth for his song
  The loud
 Shouts of the crowd;

'He asketh not world's eyes;
Not to world's ears he cries;
        Saith,—"These
    Shut, if ye please!"

'He measureth world's pleasure,
World's ease, as Saints might measure
        For hire
    Just love entire

'He asks, not grudging pain;
And knows his asking vain,
        And cries—
    "Love! Love!" and dies,

'In guerdon of long duty,
Unowned by Love or Beauty;
        And goes—
    Tell, tell, who knows!

'Aliens from Heaven's worth,
Fine beasts who nose i' the earth,
        Do there
    Reward prepare.

'But are *his* great desires
Food but for nether fires?
        Ah me,
    A mystery!

'Can it be his alone,
To find when all is known,
        That what
    He solely sought

'Is lost, and thereto lost
All that its seeking cost?
        That he
        Must finally,

'Through sacrificial tears,
And anchoretic years,
        Tryst
        With the sensualist?'

So ask; and if they tell
The secret terrible,
        Good friend,
        I pray thee send

Some high gold embassage
To teach my unripe age.
        Tell!
        Lest my feet walk hell.

A CORYMBUS FOR AUTUMN

HEARKEN my chant, 'tis
　　As a Bacchante's,
A grape-spurt, a vine-splash, a tossed tress, flown vaunt 'tis'
　　Suffer my singing,
Gipsy of Seasons, ere thou go winging;
　　Ere Winter throws
　　His slaking snows
In thy feasting-flagon's impurpurate glows!
The sopped sun—toper as ever drank hard—
　　Stares foolish, hazed,
　　Rubicund, dazed,
Totty with thine October tankard.
Tanned maiden! with cheeks like apples russet,
　And breast a brown agaric faint-flushing at tip,
And a mouth too red for the moon to buss it
　But her cheek unvow its vestalship;
　　Thy mists enclip
Her steel-clear circuit illuminous,
　　Until it crust
　　Rubiginous
With the glorious gules of a glowing rust.

Far other saw we, other indeed,
　The crescent moon, in the May-days dead,
　Fly up with its slender white wings spread
Out of its nest in the sea's waved mead.

How are the veins of thee, Autumn, laden?
     Umbered juices,
     And pulpèd oozes
    Pappy out of the cherry-bruises,
Froth the veins of thee, wild, wild maiden!
     With hair that musters
     In globèd clusters,
    In tumbling clusters, like swarty grapes,
Round thy brow and thine ears o'ershaden;
With the burning darkness of eyes like pansies,
     Like velvet pansies
     Wherethrough escapes
The splendid might of thy conflagrate fancies;
    With robe gold-tawny not hiding the shapes
      Of the feet whereunto it falleth down,
     Thy naked feet unsandallèd;
With robe gold-tawny that does not veil
     Feet where the red
     Is meshed in the brown,
Like a rubied sun in a Venice-sail.

The wassailous heart of the Year is thine!
His Bacchic fingers disentwine
     His coronal
     At thy festival;
His revelling fingers disentwine
     Leaf, flower, and all,
     And let them fall
Blossom and all in thy wavering wine.
The Summer looks out from her brazen tower,
    Through the flashing bars of July,
Waiting thy ripened golden shower;
    Whereof there cometh, with sandals fleet,

The North-west flying viewlessly,
With a sword to sheer, and untameable feet,
And the gorgon-head of the Winter shown
To stiffen the gazing earth as stone.

In crystal Heaven's magic sphere
Poised in the palm of thy fervid hand,
Thou seest the enchanted shows appear
That stain Favonian firmament;
Richer than ever the Occident
Gave up to bygone Summer's wand.
Day's dying dragon lies drooping his crest,
Panting red pants into the West.
Or the butterfly sunset claps its wings
With flitter alit on the swinging blossom,
The gusty blossom, that tosses and swings,
Of the sea with its blown and ruffled bosom;
Its ruffled bosom wherethrough the wind sings
Till the crispèd petals are loosened and strown
Overblown, on the sand;
Shed, curling as dead
Rose-leaves curl, on the fleckèd strand.

Or higher, holier, saintlier when, as now,
All Nature sacerdotal seems, and thou.
The calm hour strikes on yon golden gong,
In tones of floating and mellow light
A spreading summons to even-song:
See how there
The cowlèd Night
Kneels on the Eastern sanctuary-stair.
What is this feel of incense everywhere?
Clings it round folds of the blanch-amiced clouds,

Upwafted by the solemn thurifer,
      The mighty Spirit unknown,
That swingeth the slow earth before the embannered
    Throne?
  Or is't the Season under all these shrouds
Of light, and sense, and silence, makes her known
      A presence everywhere,
      An inarticulate prayer,
A hand on the soothed tresses of the air?
      But there is one hour scant
Of this Titanian, pirmal liturgy;
      As there is but one hour for me and thee,
    Autumn, for thee and thine hierophant,
      Of this grave-ending chant.
      Round the earth still and stark
Heaven's death-lights kindle, yellow spark by spark,
Beneath the dreadful catafalque of the dark.

      And I had ended there:
But a great wind blew all the stars to flare,
And cried, 'I sweep the path before the moon!
Tarry ye now the coming of the moon,
      For she is coming soon';
Then died before the coming of the moon.
And she came forth upon the trepidant air,
      In vesture unimagined-fair,
      Woven as woof of flag-lilies;
      And curdled as of flag-lilies
      The vapour at the feet of her,
And a haze about her tinged in fainter wise;
    As if she had trodden the stars in press,
    Till the gold wine spurted over her dress,
    Till the gold wine gushed out round her feet;

Spouted over her stainèd wear,
And bubbled in golden froth at her feet,
And hung like a whirlpool's mist round her.

Still, mighty Season, do I see't,
Thy sway is still majestical!
Thou hold'st of God, by title sure,
Thine indefeasible investiture,
And that right round thy locks are native to;
The heavens upon thy brow imperial,
This huge terrene thy ball,
And o'er thy shoulders thrown wide air's depending pail.
What if thine earth be blear and bleak of hue?
Still, still the skies are sweet!
Still, Season, still thou hast thy triumphs there!
How have I, unaware,
Forgetful of my strain inaugural,
Cleft the great rondure of thy reign complete,
Yielding thee half, who hast indeed the all?
I will not think thy sovereignty begun
But with the shepherd Sun
That washes in the sea the stars' gold fleeces;
Or that with Day it ceases,
Who sets his burning lips to the salt brine,
And purples it to wine;
While I behold how ermined Artemis
Ordainèd weed must wear,
And toil thy business;
Who witness am of her,
Her too in autumn turned a vintager;
And, laden with its lampèd clusters bright,
The fiery·fruited vineyard of this night.

ECCLESIASTICAL BALLADS

I

THE VETERAN OF HEAVEN

O CAPTAIN of the wars, whence won Ye so great scars?
  In what fight did Ye smite, and what manner was the foe?
Was it on a day of rout they compassed Thee about,
  Or gat Ye these adornings when Ye wrought their
    overthrow?

' 'Twas on a day of rout they girded Me about,
  They wounded all My brow, and they smote Me through
    the side:
My hand held no sword when I met their armèd horde,
  And the conqueror fell down, and the Conquered bruised
    his pride.'

What is this, unheard before, that the Unarmed makes war,
  And the Slain hath the gain, and the Victor hath the
    rout?
What wars, then, are these, and what the enemies,
  Strange Chief, with the scars of Thy conquest trenched
    about?

'The Prince I drave forth held the Mount of the North,
  Girt with the guards of flame that roll round the pole.

117

I drave him with My wars from all his fortress-stars,
  And the sea of death divided that My march might strike
    its goal.

'In the heart of Northern Guard, many a great dæmonian
      sword
  Burns as it turns round the Mount occult, apart:
There is given him power and place still for some certain
      days,
    And his name would turn the Sun's blood back upon its
      heart.'

What is *Thy* Name? Oh, show!—'My Name ye may not
      know;
  'Tis a going forth with banners, and a baring of much
      swords:
But My titles that are high, are they not upon My thigh?
  "King of Kings!" are the words, "Lord of Lords!";
    It is written "King of Kings, Lord of Lords.

II

LILIUM REGIS

O LILY of the King! low lies thy silver wing,
  And long has been the hour of thine unqueening;
And thy scent of Paradise on the night-wind spills its sighs,
  Nor any take the secrets of its meaning.
O Lily of the King! I speak a heavy thing,
  O patience, most sorrowful of daughters!
Lo, the hour is at hand for the troubling of the land,
  And red shall be the breaking of the waters.

Sit fast upon thy stalk, when the blast shall with thee talk,
    With the mercies of the King for thine awning;
And the just understand that thine hour is at hand,
    Thine hour at hand with power in the dawning.
When the nations lie in blood, and their kings a broken
        brood,
    Look up, O most sorrowful of daughters!
Lift up thy head and hark what sounds are in the dark,
    For His feet are coming to thee on the waters!

O Lily of the King! I shall not see, that sing,
    I shall not see the hour of thy queening!
But my Song shall see, and wake like a flower that dawn-
        winds shake,
    And sigh with joy the odours of its meaning.
O Lily of the King, remember then the thing
    That this dead mouth sang; and thy daughters,
As they dance before His way, sing there on the Day
    What I sang when the Night was on the waters!

TRANSLATIONS

A SUNSET

FROM HUGO'S 'FEUILLES D'AUTOMNE'

I LOVE the evenings, passionless and fair, I love the evens,
Whether old manor-fronts their ray with golden fulgence
    leavens,
      In numerous leafage bosomed close;
Whether the mist in reefs of fire extend its reaches sheer,
Or a hundred sunbeams splinter in an azure atmosphere
      On cloudy archipelagos.

Oh gaze ye on the firmament! a hundred clouds in motion,
Up-piled in the immense sublime beneath the winds'
    commotion,
      Their unimagined shapes accord:
Under their waves at intervals flames a pale levin through,
As if some giant of the air amid the vapours drew
      A sudden elemental sword.

The sun at bay with splendid thrusts still keeps the sullen
    fold;
And momently at distance sets, as a cupola of gold,
      The thatched roof of a cot a-glance;
Or on the blurred horizon joins his battle with the haze;
Or pools the glooming fields about with inter-isolate blaze,
      Great moveless meres of radiance.

Then mark you how there hangs athwart the firmament's
    swept track,
Yonder, a mighty crocodile with vast irradiant back,
      A triple row of pointed teeth?
Under its burnished belly slips a ray of eventide,
The flickerings of a hundred glowing clouds its tenebrous
    side
      With scales of golden mail ensheathe.

Then mounts a palace, then the air vibrates—the vision flees.
Confounded to its base, the fearful cloudy edifice
      Ruins immense in mounded wrack:
Afar the fragments strew the sky, and each envermeiled
    cone
Hangeth, peak downward, overhead, like mountains over-
    thrown
      When the earthquake heaves its hugy back.

These vapours, with their leaden, golden, iron, bronzèd
    glows,
Where the hurricane, the waterspout, thunder, and hell
    repose,
      Muttering hoarse dreams of destined harms,—
'Tis God who hangs their multitude amid the skiey deep,
As a warrior that suspendeth from the roof-tree of his keep
      His dreadful and resounding arms!

All vanishes! The sun, from topmost heaven precipitated,
Like a globe of iron which is tossed back fiery red
      Into the furnace stirred to fume,
Shocking the cloudy surges, plashed from its impetuous ire,
Even to the zenith spattereth in a flecking scud of fire
      The vaporous and inflamèd spume.

O contemplate the heavens! Whenas the vein-drawn day
    dies pale,
In every season, every place, gaze through their every veil,
      With love that has not speech for need!
Beneath their solemn beauty is a mystery infinite:
If winter hue them like a pall, or if the summer night
      Fantasy them with starry brede.

HEARD ON THE MOUNTAIN

FROM HUGO'S 'FEUILLES D'AUTOMNE'

HAVE you sometimes, calm, silent, let your tread aspirant
    rise
Up to the mountain's summit, in the presence of the skies?
Was't on the borders of the South? or on the Bretagne
    coast?
And at the basis of the mount had you the Ocean tossed?
And there, leaned o'er the wave and o'er the immeasur-
    ableness,
Calm, silent, have you harkened what it says? Lo, what
    it says!
One day at least, whereon my thought, enlicensèd to muse,
Had drooped its wing above the beachèd margent of the
    ooze,
And, plunging from the mountain height into the immensity,
Beheld upon one side the land, on the other side the sea.
I hearkened, comprehended,—never, as from those abysses,
No, never issued from a mouth, nor moved an ear such
    voice as this is!

A sound it was, at outset, immeasurable, confused,
Vaguer than is the wind among the tufted trees effused,
Full of magnificent accords, suave murmurs, sweet as is
The evensong, and mighty as the shock of panoplies
When the hoarse *mêlée* in its arms the closing squadrons
    grips,
And pants, in furious breathings, from the clarions' brazen
    lips.
Unutterable the harmony, unsearchable its deep,
Whose fluid undulations round the world a girdle keep,
And through the vasty heavens, which by its surges are
    washed young,
Its infinite volutions roll, enlarging as they throng,
Even to the profound arcane, whose ultimate chasms sombre
Its shattered flood englut with time, with space and form
    and number.
Like to another atmosphere, with thin o'erflowing robe,
The hymn eternal covers all the inundated globe:
And the world, swathed about with this investuring sym-
    phony,
Even as it trepidates in the air, so trepidates in the har-
    mony.

And pensive, I attended the ethereal lutany,
Lost within this containing voice as if within the sea.

Soon I distinguished, yet as tone which veils confuse and
    smother,
Amid this voice two voices, one commingled with the other,
Which did from off the land and seas even to the heavens
    aspire;
Chanting the universal chant in simultaneous quire

And I distinguished them amid that deep and rumorous
    sound,
As who beholds two currents thwart amid the fluctuous
    profound.

The one was of the waters; a be-radiant hymnal speech!
That was the voice o' the surges, as they parleyed each
    with each.
The other, which arose from our abode terranean,
Was sorrowful; and that, alack! the murmur was of man;
And in this mighty quire, whose chantings day and night
    resound,
Every wave had its utterance, and every man his sound.

Now, the magnificent Ocean, as I said, unbannering
A voice of joy, a voice of peace, did never stint to sing,
Most like in Sion's temples to a psaltery psaltering,
And to creation's beauty reared the great lauds of his song.
Upon the gale, upon the squall, his clamour borne along
Unpausingly arose to God in more triumphal swell;
And every one among his waves, that God alone can
    quell,
When the other of its song made end, into the singing
    pressed.
Like that majestic lion whereof Daniel was the guest,
At intervals the Ocean his tremendous murmur awed;
And, toward where the sunset fires fell shaggily and broad,
Under his golden mane, methought that I saw pass the hand
    of God.
Meanwhile, and side by side with that august fanfaronnade
The other voice, like the sudden scream of a destrier affrayed,
Like an infernal door that grates ajar its rusty throat,
Like to a bow of iron that gnarls upon an iron rote,

Grinded; and tears, and shriekings, the anathema, the lewd
    taunt,
Refusal of viaticum, refusal of the font,
And clamour, and malediction, and dread blasphemy,
    among
That hurtling crowd of rumour from the diverse human
    tongue,
Went by as who beholdeth, when the valleys thick t'ward
    night,
The long drifts of the birds of dusk pass, blackening flight
    on flight.
What was this sound whose thousand echoes vibrated
    unsleeping?
Alas! the sound was earth's and man's, for earth and man
    were weeping.

Brothers! of these two voices strange, most unimaginably,
Unceasingly regenerated, dying unceasingly,
Hearkenèd of the Eternal throughout His Eternity,
The one voice uttereth NATURE, and the other voice
    HUMANITY.

Then I alit in reverie; for my ministering sprite,
Alack! had never yet deployed a pinion of an ampler flight,
Nor ever had my shadow endured so large a day to burn:
And long I rested dreaming, contemplating turn by turn
Now that abyss obscure which lurked beneath the water's
    roll,
And now that other untemptable abyss which opened in
    my soul.
And I made question of me, to what issues are we here,
Whither should tend the thwarting threads of all this
    ravelled gear;

What doth the soul; to be or live if better worth it is;
And why the Lord, Who, only, reads within that book of
    His,
In fatal hymeneals hath eternally entwined
The vintage-chant of nature with the dirging cry of human-
    kind?

The metre of the second of these two translations is an ex-
periment. The splendid fourteen-syllable metre of Chapman I
have treated after the manner of Drydenian rhyming heroics,
with the occasional triplet, and even the occasional Alexandrine,
a treatment which can well extend, I believe, the majestic re-
sources of the metre.

AN ECHO OF VICTOR HUGO

LIFE's a veil the real has:
    All the shadows of our scene
Are but shows of things that pass
    On the other side the screen.

Time his glass sits nodding by;
    'Twixt its turn and turn a spawn
Of universes buzz and die
    Like the ephemeris of the dawn.

Turn again the wasted glass!
    Kingly crown and warrior's crest
Are not worth the blade of grass
    God fashions for the swallow's nest.

Kings must lay gold circlets down
    In God's sepulchral ante-rooms,
The wear of Heaven's the thorny crown:
    He paves His temples with their tombs.

O our towered altitudes!
  O the lustres of our thrones!
What! old Time shall have his moods
  Like Cæsars and Napoleons;

Have his towers and conquerors forth,
  Till he, weary of the toys,
Put back Rameses in the earth
  And break his Ninevehs and Troys.

The first two stanzas and the last are my own: the thoughts of the others are Victor Hugo's. The metre of the original is departed from.

MISCELLANEOUS POEMS

DREAM-TRYST

THE breaths of kissing night and day
Were mingled in the eastern Heaven:
    Throbbing with unheard melody
Shook Lyra all its star-chord seven:
    When the dusk shrunk cold, and light trod shy,
        And dawn's grey eyes were troubled grey;
    And souls went palely up the sky,
        And mine to Lucidé.

There was no change in her sweet eyes
    Since last I saw those sweet eyes shine;
There was no change in her deep heart
    Since last that deep heart knocked at mine.
        Her eyes were clear, her eyes were Hope's,
            Wherein did ever come and go
        The sparkle of the fountain-drops
            From her sweet soul below.

The chambers in the house of dreams
    Are fed with so divine an air,
That Time's hoar wings grow young therein,
    And they who walk there are most fair.

I joyed for me, I joyed for her,
  Who with the Past meet girt about:
Where our last kiss still warms the air,
  Nor can her eyes go out.

AN ARAB LOVE-SONG

THE hunchèd camels of the night*
Trouble the bright
And silver waters of the moon.
The Maiden of the Morn will soon
Through Heaven stray and sing,
Star gathering.

Now while the dark about our loves is strewn,
Light of my dark, blood of my heart, O come!
And night will catch her breath up, and be dumb.

Leave thy father, leave thy mother
And thy brother;
Leave the black tents of thy tribe apart!
Am I not thy father and thy brother,
And thy mother?
And thou—what needest with thy tribe's black tents
Who hast the red pavilion of my heart?

* Cloud-shapes observed by travellers in the East.

BUONA NOTTE

Jane Williams, in her last letter to Shelley, wrote: 'Why do you talk of never enjoying moments like the past? Are you going to join your friend Plato, or do you expect I shall do so soon? Buona Notte.' This letter was dated July 6th, and Shelley was drowned on the 8th. These verses are supposed to be addressed to Jane by the poet's spirit while his body is tossing on the waters of Spezzia.

ARIEL to Miranda:—Hear
This good-night the sea-winds bear;
And let thine unacquainted ear
Take grief for their interpreter.

Good-night! I have risen so high
Into slumber's rarity,
Not a dream can beat its feather
Through the unsustaining ether.
Let the sea-winds make avouch
How thunder summoned me to couch,
Tempest curtained me about
And turned the sun with his own hand out:
And though I toss upon my bed
My dream is not disquieted;
Nay, deep I sleep upon the deep,
And my eyes are wet, but I do not weep;
And I fell to sleep so suddenly
That my lips are moist yet—could'st thou see—
With the good-night draught I have drunk to thee.
Thou canst not wipe them; for it was Death
Damped my lips that has dried my breath.
A little while—it is not long—
The salt shall dry on them like the song.

Now know'st thou that voice desolate,—
Mourning ruined joy's estate,—
Reached thee through a closing gate.
'Go'st thou to Plato?' Ah, girl, no!
It is to Pluto that I go.

THE PASSION OF MARY

VERSES IN PASSION-TIDE

O Lady Mary, thy bright crown
  Is no mere crown of majesty;
For with the reflex of His own
  Resplendent thorns Christ circled thee.

The red rose of this Passion-tide
  Doth take a deeper hue from thee,
In the five wounds of Jesus dyed,
  And in thy bleeding thoughts, Mary!

The soldier struck a triple stroke,
  That smote thy Jesus on the tree:
He broke the Heart of Hearts, and broke
  The Saint's and Mother's heart in thee.

Thy Son went up the angels' ways,
  His passion ended; but, ah me!
Thou found'st the road of further days
  A longer way of Calvary:

On the hard cross of hope deferred
  Thou hung'st in loving agony,
Until the mortal-dreaded word
  Which chills *our* mirth, spake mirth to thee.

The angel Death from this cold tomb
  Of life did roll the stone away;
And He thou barest in thy womb
  Caught thee at last into the day,
Before the living throne of Whom
  The Lights of Heaven burning pray.

L'ENVOY

O thou who dwellest in the day!
  Behold, I pace amidst the gloom:
Darkness is ever round my way
  With little space for sunbeam-room.

Yet Christian sadness is divine
  Even as *thy* patient sadness was:
The salt tears in our life's dark wine
  Fell in it from the saving cross.

Bitter the bread of our repast;
  Yet doth a sweet the bitter leaven:
Our sorrow is the shadow cast
  Around it by the light of Heaven.

O light in Light, shine down from Heaven!

MESSAGES

WHAT shall I your true-love tell,
  Earth-forsaking maid?
What shall I your true-love tell,
  When life's spectre's laid?

'Tell him that, our side the grave,
    Maid may not conceive
Life should be so sad to have,
    That's so sad to leave!'

What shall I your true-love tell,
    When I come to him?
What shall I your true-love tell—
    Eyes growing dim!

'Tell him this, when you shall part
    From a maiden pined;
That I see him with my heart.
    Now my eyes are blind.'

What shall I your true-love tell?
    Speaking-while is scant.
What shall I your true-love tell,
    Death's white postulant?

'Tell him—love, with speech at strife,
    For last utterance saith:
I, who loved with all my life,
    Love with all my death.'

AT LORD'S

It is little I repair to the matches of the Southron folk,
Though my own red roses there may blow;
It is little I repair to the matches of the Southron folk,
Though the red roses crest the caps, I know.
For the field is full of shades as I near the shadowy coast,

And a ghostly batsman plays to the bowling of a ghost,
And I look through my tears on a soundless-clapping host
    As the run-stealers flicker to and fro,
        To and fro:—
O my Hornby and my Barlow long ago!

LOVE AND THE CHILD

    'WHY do you so clasp me,
      And draw me to your knee?
    Forsooth, you do but chafe me,
      I pray you let me be:
    I will be loved but now and then
      When it liketh me!'

    So I heard a young child,
      A thwart child, a young child
    Rebellious against love's arms,
      Make its peevish cry.

    To the tender God I turn:—
      'Pardon, Love most High!
    For I think those arms were even Thine,
      And that child was even I.'

DAPHNE

THE river-god's daughter,—the sun-god sought her,
    Sleeping with never a zephyr by her.
Under the noon he made his prey sure,
Woofed in weeds of a woven azure,
    As down he shot in a whistle of fire.

Slid off, fair daughter! her vesturing water;
    Like a cloud from the scourge of the winds fled she:
With the breath in her hair of the keen Apollo,
And feet less fleet than the feet that follow,
    She throes in his arms to a laurel-tree.

Risen out of birth's waters the soul distraught errs,
    Nor whom nor whither she flieth knows she:
With the breath in her hair of the keen Apollo,
And fleet the beat of the feet that follow,
    She throes in his arms to a poet, woe's me!

You plucked the boughed verse the poet bears—
    It shudders and bleeds as it snaps from the tree.
A love-banning love, did the god but know it,
Which barks the man about with the poet,
    And muffles his heart of mortality!

Yet I translate—ward of song's gate!—
    Perchance all ill this mystery.
We both are struck with the self-same quarrel;
We grasp the maiden, and clasp the laurel—
    Do we weep or we laugh more, *Phœbe mi?*

'His own green lays, unwithering bays,
    Gird Keats' unwithering brow,' say ye?
O fools, that is only the empty crown!
The sacred head has laid it down
    With Hob, Dick, Marian, and Margery.

ABSENCE

When music's fading's faded,
    And the rose's death is dead,
And my heart is fain of tears, because
    Mine eyes have none to shed;
        I said,
    Whence shall faith be fed?

Canst thou be what thou hast been?
    No, no more what thou hast!
Lo, all last things that I have known,
    And all that shall be last,
        Went past
With the thing thou wast!

If the petal of this Spring be
    As of the Spring that's flown,
If the thought that now is sweet is
    As the sweet thought overblown;
        Alone
Canst thou be thy self gone.

To yester-rose a richer
    The rose-spray may bear;
Thrice thousand fairer you may be,—
    But tears for the fair
        You were
When you first were fair!

Know you where they have laid her,
    Maiden May that died—
With the loves that lived not

Strowing her soft side?
I cried,
Where Has-been may hide?

To him that waiteth, all things!
Even death, if thou wait!
And they that part too early
May meet again too late:—
Ah, fate!
If meeting be too late!

And when the year new-launchèd
Shall from its wake extend
The blossomy foam of Summer,
What shall I attend,
My friend!
Flower of thee, my friend?

Sweet shall have its sorrow,
The rainbow its rain,
Loving have its leaving,
And bliss is of pain
So fain,
Ah, is she bliss or pain?

TO W. M.

O TREE of many branches! One thou hast
Thou barest not, but grafted'st on thee. Now,
Should all men's thunders break on thee, and leave
Thee reft of bough and blossom, that one branch
Shall cling to thee, my Father, Brother, Friend,
Shall cling to thee, until the end of end.

A FALLEN YEW

It seemed corrival of the world's great prime,
  Made to un-edge the scythe of Time,
    And last with stateliest rhyme.

No tender Dryad ever did indue
  That rigid chiton of rough yew,
    To fret her white flesh through:

But some god like to those grim Asgard lords,
  Who walk the fables of the hordes
    From Scandinavian fjords,

Upheaved its stubborn girth, and raised unriven,
  Against the whirl-blast and the levin,
    Defiant arms to Heaven.

When doom puffed out the stars, we might have said,
  It would decline its heavy head,
    And see the world to bed.

For this firm yew did from the vassal leas,
  And rain and air, its tributaries,
    Its revenues increase,

And levy impost on the golden sun,
  Take the blind years as they might run,
    And no fate seek or shun.

But now our yew is strook, is fallen—yea,
  Hacked like dull wood of every day
    To this and that, men say.

Never!—To Hades' shadowy shipyards gone,
  Dim barge of Dis, down Acheron
    It drops, or Lethe wan.

Stirred by its fall—poor destined bark of Dis!—
  Along my soul a bruit there is
    Of echoing images,

Reverberations of mortality:
  Spelt backward from its death, to me
    Its life reads saddenedly.

Its breast was hollowed as the tooth of eld;
  And boys, there creeping unbeheld,
    A laughing moment dwelled.

Yet they, within its very heart so crept,
  Reached not the heart that courage kept
    With winds and years beswept.

And in its boughs did close and kindly nest
  The birds, as they within its breast,
    By all its leaves caressed.

But bird nor child might touch by any art
  Each other's or the tree's hid heart,
    A whole God's breadth apart;

The breadth of God, the breadth of death and life!
  Even so, even so, in undreamed strife
    With pulseless Law, the wife,—

The sweetest wife on sweetest marriage-day,—
  Their souls at grapple in mid-way,
    Sweet to her sweet may say:

'I take you to my inmost heart, my true!'
  Ah, fool! but there is one heart you
    Shall never take him to!

The hold that falls not when the town it got,
  The heart's heart, whose immurèd plot
    Hath keys yourself keep not!

Its ports you cannot burst—you are withstood—
  For him that to your listening blood
    Sends precepts as he would.

Its gates are deaf to Love, high summoner;
  Yea, love's great warrant runs not there:
    You are your prisoner.

Yourself are with yourself the sole consortress
  In that unleaguerable fortress;
    It knows you not for portress.

Its keys are at the cincture hung of God;
  Its gates are trepidant to His nod;
    By Him its floors are trod.

And if His feet shall rock those floors in wrath,
  Or blest aspersion sleek His path,
    Is only choice it hath.

Yea, in that ultimate heart's occult abode
  To lie as in an oubliette of God,
    Or in a bower untrod,

Built by a secret Lover for His Spouse;—
  Sole choice is this your life allows,
    Sad tree, whose perishing boughs
      So few birds house!

A JUDGMENT IN HEAVEN

I have throughout this poem used an asterisk to indicate the caesura in the middle of the line, after the manner of the old Saxon section-point.

ATHWART the sod which is treading for God * the Poet
    paced with his splendid eyes;
Paradise-verdure he stately passes * to win to the Father
    of Paradise,
Through the conscious and palpitant grasses * of inter-
    tangled relucent dyes.

The angels a-play on its fields of Summer * (their wild wings
    rustled his guides' cymars)
Looked up from disport at the passing comer, * as they
    pelted each other with handfuls of stars;
And the warden-spirits with startled feet rose, * hand on
    sword, by their tethered cars.

With plumes night-tinctured englobed and cinctured * of
    Saints, his guided steps held on

To where on the far crystálline pale * of that transtellar
    Heaven there shone
The immutable crocean dawn * effusing from the Father's
    Throne.

Through the reverberant Eden-ways * the bruit of his great
    advent driven,
Back from the fulgent justle and press * with mighty echo-
    ing so was given,
As when the surly thunder smites * upon the clangèd gates
    of Heaven.

Over the bickering gonfalons, * far-ranged as for Tartarean
    wars,
Went a waver of ribbèd fire * —as night-seas on phosphoric
    bars
Like a flame-plumed fan shake slowly out * their ridgy
    reach of crumbling stars.

At length to where on His fretted Throne * sat in the heart
    of His aged dominions
The great Triune, and Mary nigh, * lit round with spears
    of their hauberked minions,
The Poet drew, in the thunderous blue * involvèd dread
    of those mounted pinions.

As in a secret and tenebrous cloud * the watcher from the
    disquiet earth
At momentary intervals * beholds from its raggèd rifts
    break forth
The flash of a golden perturbation, * the travelling threat
    of a witchèd birth;

Till heavily parts a sinister chasm, * a grisly jaw, whose
    verges soon,
Slowly and ominously filled * by the on-coming plenilune,
Supportlessly congest with fire, * and suddenly spit forth
    the moon:—

With beauty, not terror, through tangled error * of night-
    dipt plumes so burned their charge;
Swayed and parted the globing clusters * so,——disclosed
    from their kindling marge,
Roseal-chapleted, splendent-vestured, * the Poet there where
    God's light lay large.

Hu, hu! a wonder! a wonder! see, * clasping the Poet's
    glories clings
A dingy creature, even to laughter * cloaked and clad in
    patchwork things,
Shrinking close from the unused glows * of the seraphs'
    versicoloured wings.

A Rhymer, rhyming a futile rhyme, * he had crept for con-
    voy through Eden-ways
Into the shade of the Poet's glory, * darkened under his
    prevalent rays,
Fearfully hoping a distant welcome * as a poor kinsman
    of his lays.

The angels laughed with a lovely scorning: * — 'Who has
    done this sorry deed in
The garden of our Father, God? * 'mid his blossoms to
    sow this weed in?
Never our fingers knew this stuff: * not so fashion the
    looms of Eden!'

The Poet bowed his brow majestic, * searching that patch-
    work through and through,
Feeling God's lucent gazes traverse * his singing-stoling and
    spirit too:
The hallowed harpers were fain to frown * on the strange
    thing come 'mid their sacred crew.
Only the Poet that was earth * his fellow-earth and his
    own self knew.

Then the Poet rent off robe and wreath, * so as a sloughing
    serpent doth,
Laid them at the Rhymer's feet, * shed down wreath and
    raiment both,
Stood in a dim and shamèd stole, * like the tattered wing
    of a musty moth.

(*The Poet addresses his Maker*)
'Thou gav'st the weed and wreath of song, * the weed and
    wreath are solely Thine,
And this dishonest vesture * is the only vesture that is
    mine;
The life *I* textured, Thou the song: * —— *my* handicraft
    is not divine!'

(*The Poet addresses the Rhymer*)
He wrested o'er the Rhymer's head * that garmenting which
    wrought him wrong;
A flickering tissue argentine * down dripped its shivering
    silvers long:—
'Better thou wov'st thy woof of life * than thou didst weave
    thy woof of song!'

Never a chief in Saintdom was, * but turned him from the
    Poet then;
Never an eye looked mild on him * 'mid all the angel my-
    riads ten,
Save sinless Mary, and sinful Mary * —the Mary titled
    Magdalen.

'Turn yon robe,' spake Magdalen, * 'of torn bright song,
    and see and feel.'
They turned the raiment, saw and felt * what their turning
    did reveal—
All the inner surface piled * with bloodied hairs, like hairs
    of steel.

'Take, I pray, yon chaplet up, * thrown down ruddied from
    his head.'
They took the roseal chaplet up, * and they stood aston-
    ishèd:
Every leaf between their fingers, * as they bruised it, burst
    and bled.

'See his torn flesh through those rents; * see the punctures
    round his hair,
As if the chaplet-flowers had driven * deep roots in to nour-
    ish there—
Lord, who gav'st him robe and wreath, * *what* was this Thou
    gav'st for wear?'

'Fetch forth the Paradisal garb!' * spake the Father, sweet
    and low;
Drew them both by the frightened hand * where Mary's
    throne made irised bow—
'Take, Princess Mary, of thy good grace, * two spirits greater
    than they know.'

EPILOGUE TO
'A JUDGMENT IN HEAVEN'

VIRTUE may unlock hell, or even
A sin turn in the wards of Heaven,
(As ethics of the text-book go,)
So little men their own deeds know,
Or through the intricate *mêlée*
Guess witherward draws the battle-sway;
So little, if they know the deed,
Discern what therefrom shall succeed.
To wisest moralists 'tis but given
To work rough border-law of Heaven,
Within this narrow life of ours,
These marches 'twixt delimitless Powers.
Is it, if Heaven the future showed,
Is it the all-severest mode
To see ourselves with the eyes of God?
God rather grant, at His assize,
He see us not with our own eyes!

Heaven, which man's generations draws,
Nor deviates into replicas,
Must of as deep diversity
In judgement as creation be.
There is no expeditious road
To pack and label men for God,
And save them by the barrel-load.
Some may perchance, with strange surprise,
Have blundered into Paradise.
In vasty dusk of life abroad,
They fondly thought to err from God,
Nor knew the circle that they trod;

And, wandering all the night about,
Found them at morn where they set out.
Death dawned; Heaven lay in prospect wide:—
Lo! they were standing by His side!

The Rhymer a life uncomplex,
With just such cares as mortals vex,
So simply felt as all men feel,
Lived purely out to his soul's weal.
A double life the Poet lived,
And with a double burthen grieved;
The life of flesh and life of song,
The pangs to both lives that belong;
Immortal knew and mortal pain,
Who in two worlds could lose and gain,
And found immortal fruits must be
Mortal through his mortality.
The life of flesh and life of song!
If one life worked the other wrong,
What expiating agony
May for him, damned to poesy,
Shut in that little sentence be—
What deep austerities of strife—
'He lived his life.' He lived *his* life!

THE SERE OF THE LEAF

WINTER wore a flapping wind, and his beard, disentwined,
    Blew cloudy in the face of the Fall,
When a poet-soul flew South, with a singing in her mouth,
    O'er the azure Irish parting-wall. *

* Miss Katharine Tynan's visit to London, 1889.

There stood one beneath a tree whose matted greenery
    Was fruited with the songs of birds;
By the melancholy water drooped the slender sedge, its
    daughter,
    Whose silence was a sadness passing words:
        He held him very still,
        And he heard the running rill,
And the soul-voice singing blither than the birds.

All Summer the sunbeams drew the curtains from the
    dreams
    Of the rose-fay, while the sweet South wind
Lapped the silken swathing close round her virginal repose
    When night swathed folding slumbers round her mind.
Now the elf of the flower had sickened in her bower,
    And fainted in a thrill of scent;
But her lover of the South, with a moan upon his mouth,
    Caught her spirit to his arms as it went:
        Then the storms of West and North
        Sent a gusty vaward forth,
Sent a skirring desolation, and he went.

And a troop of roving gales rent the lily's silver veils,
    And tore her from her trembling leaves;
And the Autumn's smitten face flushed to a red disgrace,
    And she grieved as a captive grieves.
Once the gold-barred cage of skies with the sunset's moulted
    dyes
    Was splendorously littered at the even;
Beauty-fraught o'er shining sea, once the sun's argosy
    To rich wreck on the Western reefs was driven;
        Now the sun, in Indian pall,
        Treads the russet-amber fall
From the ruined trees of Heaven.

Too soon fails the light, and the swart boar, night,
    Gores to death the bleeding day;
And the dusk has no more a calm at its core,
    But is turbid with obscene array.
For the cloud, a thing of ill dilating baleful o'er the hill,
    Spreads a bulk like a huge Afreet
Drifting in gigantic sloth, or a murky behemoth,
    For the moon to set her silver feet;
        For the moon's white paces,
        And its nostril for her traces,
As she urges it with wild witch feet.

And the stars, forlornly fair, shiver keenly through the air,
    All an-aching till their watch be ceased;
And the hours like maimed flies lag on, ere night hatch her
        golden dragon
    In the mold of the upheaved East.
'As the cadent languor lingers after Music droops her fin-
        gers,
    Beauty still falls dying, dying through the days;
But ah!' said he who stood in that Autumn solitude
    'Singing-soul, thou art 'lated with thy lays!
        All things that on this globe err
        Fleet into dark October,
When day and night encounter, the nights war down the
        days.

'For the song in thy mouth is all of the South,
    Though Winter wax in strength more and more,
And at eve with breath of malice the stained windows of
        day's palace
    Pile in shatters on the Western floor.'

But the song sank down his soul like a Naiad through her
    pool,
  He could not bid the visitant depart;
For he felt the melody make tune like a bee
  In the red rose of his heart:
    Like a Naiad in her pool
    It lay within his soul,
Like a bee in the red rose of his heart.

She sang of the shrill East fled and bitterness surceased:—
  'O the blue South wind is musical!
And the garden's drenched with scent, and my soul hath its
    content,
  This eve or any eve at all.'
On his form the blushing shames of her ruby-plumaged flames
  Flickered hotly, like a quivering crimson snow:
'And hast thou thy content? Were some rain of it besprent
  On the soil where I am drifted to and fro,
    My soul, blown o'er the ways
    Of these arid latter days,
Would blossom like a rose of Jericho.

'I know not equipoise, only purgatorial joys,
  Grief's singing to the soul's instrument,
And forgetfulness which yet knoweth that it doth forget;
  But content—what is content?
For a harp of singeing wire, and a goblet dripping fire,
  And desires that hunt down Beauty through the Heaven
With unslackenable bounds, as the deep-mouthed thunder-
    hounds
  Bay at heel the fleeing levin,—
    The chaliced lucencies
    From pure holy-wells of eyes,
And the bliss unbarbed with pain I have given.

'Is—O framed to suffer joys!—*thine* the sweet without al-
    loys
    Of the many, who art numbered with the few?
And thy flashing breath of song, does it do *thy* lips no
    wrong,
    Nor sear them as the heats spill through?
When the welling musics rise, like tears from heart to eyes,
    Is there not a pang dissolved in them for thee?
Does not Song, like the Queen of radiant Love, Hellene,
    Float up dripping from a bitter sea?
      No tunèd metal known
      Unless stricken yields a tone,
Be it silver, or sad iron like to me.

'Yet the rhymes still roll from the bell-tower of thy soul,
    Though no tongued griefs give them vent;
If they ring to me no gladness, if *my* joy be sceptred sad-
    ness,
    I am glad, yet, for *thy* content.
Not always does the lost, 'twixt the fires of heat and frost,
    Envy those whom the healing lustres bless;
But may sometimes, in the pain of a yearning past attain,
    Thank the angels for their happiness;
      'Twixt the fire and fiery ice,
      Looking up to Paradise,
Thank the angels for their happiness.

'The heart, a censered fire whence fuming chants aspire,
    Is fed with oozèd gums of precious pain;
And unrest swings denser, denser, the fragrance from that
    censer,
    With the heart-strings for its quivering chain.
Yet 'tis vain to scale the turret of the cloud-uplifted spirit,
    And bar the immortal in, the mortal out;

For sometime unaware comes a footfall up the stair,
　And a soft knock under which no bolts are stout,
　　And lo, there pleadeth sore
　　The heart's voice at the door,
"I am your child, you may not shut me out!"

'The breath of poetry in the mind's autumnal tree
　Shakes down the saddened thoughts in singing showers,
But fallen from their stem, what part have we in them?
　"Nay," pine the trees, "they were, but are not ours."
Not for the mind's delight these serèd leaves alight,
　But, loosened by the breezes, fall they must.
What ill if they decay? yet some a little way
　May flit before deserted by the gust,
　　May touch some spirit's hair,
　　May cling one moment there,—
She turns; they tremble down. Drift o'er them, dust!'

TO STARS

You, my unrest, and Night's tranquillity,
Bringers of peace to it, and pang to me:
You that on heaven and on my heart cast fire,
To heaven a purging light, my heart unpurged desire;
Bright juts for foothold to the climbing sight
Which else must slip from the steep infinite;
Reared standards which the sequent centuries
Snatch, each from his forerunner's grasp who dies,
To lead our forlorn hope upon the skies;
Bells that from night's great bell-tower hang in gold,
Whereon God rings His changes manifold;
Meek guides and daughters to the blinded heaven

In Œdipean, remitless wandering driven;
The burning rhetoric, quenchless oratory,
Of the magniloquent and all-suasive sky;
I see and feel you—but to feel and see
How two child-eyes have dulled a firmament for me.

Once did I bring her, hurt upon her bed,
Flowers we had loved together; brought, and said:—
'I plucked them; yester-morn you liked them wild.'
And then she laid them on my eyes, and smiled.
And now, poor Stars, your fairness is not fair,
Because I cannot gather it for her;
I cannot sheave you in my arms, and say:—
'See, sweet, you liked these yester-eve; like them for *me*
    to-day!'

She has no care, my Stars, of you or me;
She has no care, we tire her speedily;
She has no care, because she cannot see—
She cannot see, who sees not past her sight.
We are set too high, we tire her with our height:
Her years are small, and ill to strain above.
She may not love us: wherefore keep we love
To her who may not love us—you and I?
And yet you thrill down towards her, even as I,
With all your golden eloquence held in mute.
We may not plead, we may not plead our suit;
Our wingèd love must beat against its bars:
For should she enter once within those guarding bars,
Our love would do her hurt—oh, think of that, my Stars!

LINES FOR A DRAWING OF OUR LADY OF THE NIGHT

THIS, could I paint my inward sight,
This were Our Lady of the Night:

She bears on her front's lucency
The starlight of her purity:

For as the white rays of that star
The union of all colours are,

She sums all virtues that may be
In her sweet light of purity.

The mantle which she holds on high
Is the great mantle of the sky.

Think, O sick toiler, when the night
Comes on thee, sad and infinite,

Think, sometimes, 'tis our own Lady
Spreads her blue mantle over thee,

And folds the earth, a wearied thing,
Beneath its gentle shadowing;

Then rest a little; and in sleep
Forget to weep, forget to weep!

ORISON-TRYST

SHE told me, in the morning her white thought
Did beat to Godward, like a carrier-dove,
My name beneath its wing. And I—how long!—
That, like a bubble from a water-flower
Released as it withdraws itself up-curled
Into the nightly lake, her sighèd name
So loosened from my sleepward-sinking heart;
And in the morning did like Phosphor set it
To lead the vanward of my orient soul
When it storms Heaven; and did all alone,
Methought, upon the live coals of my love
Those distillations of rich memory cast
To feed the fumes of prayer:—oh! I was then
Like one who, dreaming solitude, awakes
In sobbing from his dream; and, straining arms
That ache for their own void, with sudden shock
Takes a dear form beside him.
                           Now, when light
Pricks at my lids, I never rouse but think—
'Is 't orison-time with her?'—And then my hand
Presses thy letters in my pulses shook;
Where, neighboured on my heart with those pure lines
In amity of kindred pureness, lies
Image of Her conceived Immaculate;
And on the purple inward, thine,—ah! thine
O' the purple-linèd side.
                        And I do set
Tryst with thy soul in its own Paradise;
As lovers of an earthly rate that use,
In severance, for their sweet messages
Some concave of a tree, and do their hearts

Enharbour in its continent heart—I drop
My message in the hollow breast of God.
Thy name is known in Heaven; yea, Heaven is weary
With the reverberation of thy name;
I fill with it the gap between two sleeps,
The inter-pause of dream: hell's gates have learned
To shake in it; and their fierce forayers
Before the iterate echoing recoil,
In armèd watches when my preparate soul
(A war-cry in the alarums of the Night)
Conjoins thy name with Hers, Auxiliatrix.

'WHERETO ART THOU COME?'

'FRIEND, whereto art thou come?' Thus Verity;
Of each that to the world's sad Olivet
Comes with no multitude, but alone by night,
Lit with the one torch of his lifted soul,
Seeking her that he may lay hands on her;
Thus: and waits answer from the mouth of deed.
Truth is a maid, whom men woo diversely;
This, as a spouse; that, as a light-o'-love,
To know, and having known, to make his brag.
But woe to him that takes the immortal kiss,
And not estates her in his housing life,
Mother of all his seed! So he betrays,
Not Truth, the unbetrayable, but himself:
And with his kiss's rated traitor-craft
The Haceldama of a plot of days
He buys, to consummate his Judasry
Therein with Judas' guerdon of despair.

SONG OF THE HOURS

SCENE: *Before the Palace of the Sun, into which a god has just passed as the guest of Hyperion.* TIME: *Dawn. The Hours of Night and Day advance on each other as the gates close.*

MORNING HOURS

IN curbed expanses our wheeling dances
   Meet from the left and right;
Under this vaporous awning
   Tarrying awhile in our flight,
Waiting the day's advances,
   We, the children of light,
Clasp you on verge of the dawning,
   Sisters of Even and Night!

CHORUS

We who lash from the way of the sun
   With the whip of the winds the thronging clouds,
Who puff out the lights of the stars, or run
   To scare dreams back to their shrouds,
Or tiar the temples of Heaven
   With a crystalline gleam of showers;

EVENING HOURS

While to flit with the soft moth, Even,
   Round the lamp of the day is ours;

NIGHT HOURS

And ours with her crescent argentine,
    To make Night's forehead fair,
To wheel up her throne of the earth, and twine
    The daffodils in her hair;

ALL

We, moulted as plumes are,
    From the wings whereon Time is borne;

MORNING HOURS

We, buds who in blossoming foretell
    The date when our leaves shall be torn;

NIGHT HOURS

We, knowing our dooms are to plunge with the gloom's
    car
Down the steep ruin of morn;

ALL

We hail thee, Immortal!
We robes of Life, mouldering while worn.

NIGHT HOURS

Sea-birds, winging o'er sea calm-strewn
  To the lure of the beacon-stars, are we,
O'er the foamy wake of the white-sailed moon,
  Which to men is the Galaxy.

MORNING HOURS

Our eyes, through our pinions folden,
  By the filtered flame are teased
As we bow when the sun makes golden
  Earthquake in the East.

EVENING HOURS

And *we* shake on the sky a dusted fire
  From the ripened sunset's anther,
While the flecked main, drowsing in gorged desire,
  Purrs like an outstretched panther.

MORNING HOURS

O'er the dead moon-maid
  We draw softly the day's white pall;
And our children the Moments we see as
  In drops of the dew they fall,
Or on light plumes laid they shoot the cascade
  Of colours some Heaven's bow call;

ALL

And we sing, Guest, to thee, as
Thou pacest the crystal-paved hall!

We, while the sun with his hid chain swings
　　Like a censer around him the blossom-sweet earth,
Who dare the lark with our passionate wings,
　　And its mirth with our masterless mirth;
　　Or—when that flying laughter
　　　Has sunk and died away
　　Which beat against Heaven's rafter—
　　　Who vex the clear eyes of day,
Who weave for the sky in the loom of the cloud
　　A mantle of waving rain,
We, whose hair is jewelled with joys, or bowed
　　Under veilings of misty pain;
　　We hymn thee at leaving
Who strew thy feet's coming, O Guest!
We, the linked cincture which girdles
Mortality's feverous breast,
Who heave in its heaving, who grieve in its grieving,
　　Are restless in its unrest;
Our beings unstirred else
　　Were it not for the bosom they pressed.

We see the wind, like a light swift leopard
　　Leap on the flocks of the cloud that flee,
As we follow the feet of the radiant shepherd
　　Whose bright sheep drink of the sea.
　　When that drunken Titan the Thunder
　　　Stumbles through staggered Heaven,
　　And spills on the scorched earth under

The fiery wine of the levin,
With our mystic measure of rhythmic motion
  We charm him in snorting sleep,
While round him the sun enchants from ocean
    The walls of a cloudy keep.
    Beneath the deep umbers
Of night as we watch and hark,
  The dim-wingèd dreams which feed on
The blossoms of day we mark,
As in murmurous numbers they swarm to the slumbers
  That cell the hive of the dark;
And life shakes, a reed on
  Our tide, in the death-wind stark.

Time, Eternity's fountain, whose waters
  Fall back thither from whence they rose,
Deweth with us, its showery daughters,
  The Life that is green in its flows.
But whether in grief or mirth we shower,
  We make not the thing we breed,
For what may come of the passing Hour
  Is what was hid in the seed.
    And now as wakes,
      Like love in its first blind guesses,
    Or a snake just stirring its coils,
      Sweet tune into half-caresses,
    Before the sun shakes the clinging flakes
      Of gloom from his spouting tresses,
    Let winds have toils
      To catch at our fluttering dresses!
Winter, that numbeth the throstle and stilled wren,
  Has keen frost-edges our plumes to pare,

Till we break, with the Summer's laughing children,
  Over the fields of air.
    While the winds in their tricksome courses
      The snowy steeds vault upon
    That are foaled of the white sea-horses
      And washed in the streams of the sun.
Thaw, O thaw the enchanted throbbings
  Curdled at Music's heart;
Tread she her grapes till from their englobings
  The melodies spurt and smart!
    We fleet as a rain,
      Nor yearn for the being men own,
    With whom is naught beginneth
      Or endeth without some moan;
    We soar to our zenith
      And are panglessly overblown.

Yet, if the roots of the truth were bare,
  Our transience is only a mortal seeming;
Fond men, we are fixed as a still despair,
  And we fleet but in your dreaming.
    We are columns in Time's hall, mortals,
      Wherethrough Life hurrieth;
    You pass in at birth's wide portals,
      And out at the postern of death.
As you chase down the vista your dream or your
    love
  The swift pillars race you by,
And you think it is we who move, who move,—
  It is you who die, who die!
    O firmament, even
      You pass, by whose fixture man voweth;
    God breathes you forth as a bubble

And shall suck you back into His mouth!
Through earth, sea, and heaven a doom shall be
    driven,
    And, sown in the furrows it plougheth,
As fire bursts from stubble
    Shall spring the new wonders none troweth.

The bowed East lifteth the dripping sun,
    A golden cup, to the lips of Night,
Over whose cheek in flushes run
    The heats of the liquid light.

MORNING HOURS

To our very pinions' ridge
    We tremble expectantly;—
Is it ready, the burnished bridge
    We must cast for our King o'er the sea?
And who will kneel with sunbeam-slips
    To dry the flowers' sweet eyes?
Who touch with fire her finger-tips
    For the lamp of the grape, as she flies?

ALL

List, list to the prances, his chariot advances,
    It comes in a dust of light!
From under our brightening awning
    We wheel in a diverse flight:
Yet the hands we unclasp, as our dances
    Sweep off to the left and the right,
Are but loosed on the verge of the dawning
    To join on the verge of the night.

PASTORAL

PAN-IMBUED
Tempe wood,
  Pretty player's sporting-place;
    Tempe wood's
    Solitude's
  Everywhere a courting-place.
    Kiss me, sweet
    Gipsy fleet,
  Though a kissed maid hath her **red**;
    Kisses grow—
    Trust me so—
  Faster than they're gatherèd!
  I will flute a tune
    On the pipes of ivory;
  All long noon
    Piping of a melody;
  A merry, merry, merry, merry,
    Merry, merry melody.
Dance, ho! foot it so! Feat fleets the melody!

    Let the wise
    Say, youth dies;—
  'Tis for pleasure's mending, Sweet!
    Kisses are
    Costlier far,
  That they have an ending, Sweet!
    Half a kiss's
    Dainty bliss is
  From the day of kiss-no-more;
    When we shall,
    Roseal

Lass, do this and this no more!
And we pipe a tune
    On the pipes of ivory;
All long noon
    Fluting of a melody:—
A merry, merry, merry, merry,
    Merry, merry melody.
Dance, ho! trip it so!   Feat fleets the melody!

My love must
Be to trust,
While you safely fold me close:
    Yours will smile
    A kissing-while,
For the hours I hold you close.
    Maiden gold!
    Clipping bold
Here the truest mintage is:
    Lips will bear
    But, I swear,
In the press their vintages!
I will flute a tune
    On the pipes of ivory;
All long noon
    Piping of a melody:—
A merry, merry, merry, merry,
    Merry, merry melody.
Dance, ho! foot it so!   Feat fleets the melody!

PAST THINKING OF SOLOMON

Remember thy Creator in the days of thy youth, before the years draw nigh of which thou shalt say: They please me not; before the sun, and the light, and the moon, and the stars be darkened, and the clouds return after the rain.
Ecclesiastes.

Wise-Unto-Hell Ecclesiast,
Who siev'dst life to the gritted last!

This thy sting, thy darkness, Mage—
Cloud upon sun, upon youth age?

Now is come a darker thing,
And is come a colder sting,

Unto us, who find the womb
Opes on the courtyard of the tomb.

Now in this fuliginous
City of flesh our sires for us

Darkly built, the sun at prime
Is hidden, and betwixt the time

Of day and night is variance none,
Who know not altern moon and sun;

Whose deposed heaven through dungeon-bars
Looks down blinded of its stars.

Yea, in the days of youth, God wot,
Now we say: They please me not.

A DEAD ASTRONOMER

STEPHEN PERRY, S.J.

STARRY amorist, starward gone,
Thou art—what thou didst gaze upon!
Passed through thy golden garden's bars,
Thou seest the Gardener of the Stars.

She, about whose moonèd brows
Seven stars make seven glows,
Seven lights for seven woes;
She, like thine own Galaxy,
All lustres in one purity:—
What said'st thou, Astronomer,
When thou did'st discover *her?*
When thy hand its tube let fall,
Thou found'st the fairest Star of all!

CHEATED ELSIE

ELSIE was a maiden fair
   As the sun
   Shone upon:
Born to teach her swains despair
By smiling on them every one;
Born to win all hearts to her
Just because herself had none;
All the day she had no care,
For she was a maiden fair
   As the sun
   Shone upon,
Heartless as the brooks that run.

All the maids, with envy tart,
Sneering said, 'She has no heart.'
All the youths, with bitter smart,
Sighing said, 'She has no heart!'
  Could she care
For their sneers or their despair
When she was a maiden fair
  As the sun
  Shone upon,
Heartless as the brooks that run?

But one day whenas she stood
  In a wood
Haunted by the fairy brood,
Did she view, or dream she viewed
  In a vision's
  Wild misprisions,
How a pedlar, dry and rude
As a crook'd branch taking flesh,
Caught the spirit in a mesh,
Singing of—'What is't ye lack?'
  Wizard-pack
  On twisted back,
 Still he sang, 'What is't ye lack?

'Lack ye land or lack ye gold,
What I give, I give unsold;
Lack ye wisdom, lack ye beauty,
  To your suit he
Gives unpaid, the pedlar old!'

Fairies.

Beware, beware! the gifts he gives
One pays for, sweetheart, while one lives!

Elsie.

What is it the maidens say
That I lack?

Pedlar.

By this bright day,
Can so fair a maiden lack?
Maid so sweet
Should be complete.

Elsie.

Yet a thing they say I lack.
In thy pack,—
Pedlar, tell—
Hast thou ever a heart to sell?

Pedlar.

Yea, a heart I have, as tender
As the mood of evening air.

Elsie.

Name thy price!

Pedlar.

The price, by Sorrow!
Only is, the heart to wear.

Elsie.

Not great the price, as was my fear.

Fairies.

So cheap a price was ne'er so dear.
   Beware, beware,
   O rash and fair!
   The gifts he gives,
Sweetheart, one pays for while one lives!

Scarce the present did she take,
When the heart began to ache.

Elsie.

Ah, what is this?   Take back thy gift!
   I had not, and I knew no lack;
Now I have, I lack for ever!

Fairies.

   The gifts he gives, he takes not back.

Elsie.

Ah! why the present did I take,
And knew not that a heart would ache?

Fairies.

Ache! and is that all thy sorrow?—
Beware, beware—a heart will break!

THE FAIR INCONSTANT

Dost thou still hope thou shalt be fair,
   When no more fair to me?
Or those that by thee taken were

Hold their captivity?
Is this thy confidence? No, no;
Trust it not; it can not be so.

But thou too late, too late shalt find
 'Twas I that made thee fair;
Thy beauties never from thy mind
 But from my loving were;
And those delights that did thee stole
Confessed the vicinage of my soul.

The rosy reflex of my heart
 Did thy pale cheek attire;
And what I was, not what thou art,
 Did gazers-on admire.
Go, and too late thou shalt confess
I looked thee into loveliness!

THREATENED TEARS

Do not loose those rains thy wet
Eyes, my Fair, unsurely threat;
Do not, Sweet, do not so!
Thou canst not have a single woe,
But this sad and doubtful weather
Overcasts us both together.
In the aspèct of those known eyes
My soul's a captain weatherwise.
Ah me! what presages it sees
In those watery Hyades.

THE HOUSE OF SORROWS *

I

Of the white purity
    They wrought my wedding-dress,
Inwoven silverly—
    For tears, as I do guess.
Oh, why did they with tears inweave my marriage-dress?

A girl, I did espouse
    Destiny, grief, and fears;
The love of Austria's house
    And its ancestral years
I learned; and my salt eyes grew erudite in tears.

Devote our tragic line—
    One to his rebel's aim,
One to his ignorant brine,
    One to the eyeless flame:
Who should be skilled to weep but I, O Christ's dear Dame?

[* In the opening stanzas the Empress Elizabeth of Austria addresses Our Lady, then the 'Dark Fool' Death, and finally the Son of Sorrows, in allusion to the griefs of her own and her husband's line: the shooting of Maximilian of Mexico, her sister's burning at the Paris Bazar de la Charité, the drowning of the Archduke John and of the mad King of Bavaria, and the tragedy of the Crown Prince Rudolph. Her own assassination was the immediate occasion of these verses; and the traditional offering of her wedding-wreath to a Madonna-shrine and the making of her wedding-gown into priestly vestments elucidate other references in the text.]

Give one more to the fire,
   One more for water keep:
O Death, wilt thou not tire?
   Still Austria must thou reap?
Can I have plummetless tears, that still thou bidd'st 'Weep,
   weep!'?

No—thou at length with me
   Too far, Dark Fool, hast gone!
One costly cruelty
   Voids thy dominion:
I am drained to the uttermost tear: O Rudolph, O my son!

Take this woof of sorrows,
   Son of all Women's Tears!
I am not for the morrows,
   I am dead with the dead years.
Lo, I vest Thee, Christ, with my woven tears!

My bridal wreath take thou,
   Mary! Take Thou, O Christ,
My bridal garment! Now
   Is all my fate sufficed,
And, robed and garlanded, the victim sacrificed.

II

The Son of Weeping heard,
   The gift benignly saw;
The Women's Pitier heard.
   Together, by hid law,
The life-gashed heart, the assassin's healing poniard, draw.

Too long that consummation
　　The obdurate seasons thwart;
Too long were the sharp consolation
　　And her breast apart;—
The remedy of steel has gone home to her sick heart.

Her breast, dishabited,
　　Revealed, her heart above,
A little blot of red,—
　　Death's reverent sign to approve
He had sealed up that royal tomb of martyred love.

Now, Death, if thou wouldst show
　　Some ruth still left in store,
Guide thou the armèd blow
　　To strike one bosom more,
Where any blow were pity, to this it struck before!

INSENTIENCE

O sweet is Love, and sweet is Lack!
　　But is there any charm
When Lack from round the neck of Love
　　Drops her languid arm?

Weary, I no longer love,
　　Weary, no more lack;
O for a pang, that listless Loss
Might wake, and, with a playmate's voice,
　　Call the tired Love back!

ENVOY

Go, songs, for ended is our brief, sweet play;
  Go, children of swift joy and tardy sorrow:
And some are sung, and that was yesterday,
  And some unsung, and that may be to-morrow.

Go forth; and if it be o'er stony way,
  Old joy can lend what newer grief must borrow:
And it was sweet, and that was yesterday,
  And sweet is sweet, though purchasèd with sorrow.

Go, songs, and come not back from your far way:
  And if men ask you why ye smile and sorrow,
Tell them ye grieve, for your hearts know To-day,
  Tell them ye smile, for your eyes know To-morrow.

DEDICATION OF NEW POEMS

(1897)

To Coventry Patmore

Lo, my book thinks to look Time's leaguer **down**,
Under the banner of your spread renown!
Or if these levies of impuissant rhyme
Fall to the overthrow of assaulting Time,
Yet this one page shall fend oblivious shame,
Armed with your crested and prevailing **Name.**

This dedication was written while the dear friend and great Poet to whom it was addressed yet lived. It is left as he saw it—the last verses of mine that were to pass under his eyes.

SIGHT AND INSIGHT

Wisdom is easily seen by them that love her, and is found by
them that seek her.
To think therefore upon her is perfect understanding.

WISDOM, vi.

THE MISTRESS OF VISION

I

SECRET was the garden;
Set i' the pathless awe
Where no star its breath can draw.
Life, that is its warden,
Sits behind the fosse of death. Mine eyes saw not, and I
  saw.

II

It was a mazeful wonder;
Thrice three times it was enwalled
With an emerald—
Sealèd so asunder.
All its birds in middle air hung a-dream, their music
  thralled.

III

The Lady of fair weeping,
At the garden's core,
Sang a song of sweet and sore
And the after-sleeping;
In the land of Luthany, and the tracts of Elenore.

IV

With sweet-pangèd singing,
Sang she through a dream-night's day;
That the bowers might stay,
Birds bate their winging,
Nor the wall of emerald float in wreathèd haze away.

V

The lily kept its gleaming,
In her tears (divine conservers!)
Washèd with sad art;
And the flowers of dreaming
Palèd not their fervours,
For her blood flowed through their nervures;
And the roses were most red, for she dipt them in her heart.

VI

There was never moon,
Save the white sufficing woman:
Light most heavenly-human—
Like the unseen form of sound,

Sensed invisibly in tune,—
With a sun-derivèd stole
Did inaureole
All her lovely body round;
Lovelily her lucid body with that light was interstrewn.

VII

The sun which lit that garden wholly,
Low and vibrant visible,
Tempered glory woke;
And it seemèd solely
Like a silver thurible
Solemnly swung, slowly,
Fuming clouds of golden fire, for a cloud of incense-smoke

VIII

But woe's me, and woe's me,
For the secrets of her eyes!
In my visions fearfully
They are ever shown to be
As fringèd pools, whereof each lies
Pallid-dark beneath the skies
Of a night that is
But one blear necropolis.
And her eyes a little tremble, in the wind of her own sighs.

IX

Many changes rise on
Their phantasmal mysteries.
They grow to an horizon
Where earth and heaven meet;
And like a wing that dies on
The vague twilight-verges,
Many a sinking dream doth fleet
Lessening down their secrecies.
And, as dusk with day converges,
Their orbs are troublously
Over-gloomed and over-glowed with hope and fear of things
    to be.

X

There is a peak on Himalay,
And on the peak undeluged snow,
And on the snow not eagles stray;
There if your strong feet could go,—
Looking over tow'rd Cathay
From the never-deluged snow—
Farthest ken might not survey
Where the peoples underground dwell whom antique fables
    know.

XI

East, ah, east of Himalay,
Dwell the nations underground;
Hiding from the shock of Day,
For the sun's uprising-sound:

Dare not issue from the ground
At the tumults of the Day,
So fearfully the sun doth sound
Clanging up beyond Cathay;
For the great earthquaking sunrise rolling up beyond Cathay.

XII

Lend me, O lend me
The terrors of that sound,
That its music may attend me,
Wrap my chant in thunders round;
While I tell the ancient secrets in that Lady's singing found.

XIII

On Ararat there grew a vine;
When Asia from her bathing rose,
Our first sailor made a twine
Thereof for his prefiguring brows.
Canst divine
Where, upon our dusty earth, of that vine a cluster grows?

XIV

On Golgotha there grew a thorn
Round the long-prefigured Brows.
Mourn, O mourn!
For the vine have we the spine? Is this all the Heaven
allows?

XV

On Calvary was shook a spear;
Press the point into thy heart—
Joy and fear!
All the spines upon the thorn into curling tendrils start.

XVI

O dismay!
I, a wingless mortal, sporting
With the tresses of the sun?
I, that dare my hand to lay
On the thunder in its snorting?
Ere begun,
Falls my singed song down the sky, even the old Icarian way.

XVII

From the fall precipitant
These dim snatches of her chant
Only have remainèd mine;—
That from spear and thorn alone
May be grown
For the front of saint or singer any divinizing twine.

XVIII

Her song said that no springing
Paradise but evermore
Hangeth on a singing
That has chords of weeping,

And that sings the after-sleeping
To souls which wake too sore.
'But woe the singer, woe!' she said; 'beyond the dead his
    singing-lore,
      All its art of sweet and sore,
      He learns, in Elenore!"

XIX

Where is the land of Luthany,
Where is the tract of Elenore?
I am bound therefor.

XX

'Pierce thy heart to find the key;
  With thee take
Only what none else would keep;
Learn to dream when thou dost wake,
Learn to wake when thou dost sleep;
Learn to water joy with tears,
Learn from fears to vanquish fears,
To hope, for thou dar'st not despair,
Exult, for that thou dar'st not grieve;
Plough thou the rock until it bear;
Know, for thou else couldst not believe;
Lose, that the lost thou may'st receive;
Die, for none other way canst live.
When earth and heaven lay down their veil,
And that apocalypse turns thee pale;
When thy seeing blindeth thee

To what thy fellow-mortals see;
When their sight to thee is sightless;
Their living, death; their light, most lightless;
Search no more—
Pass the gates of Luthany, tread the region Elenore."

XXI

Where is the land of Luthany,
And where the region Elenore?
I do faint therefor.

XXII

'When to the new eyes of thee
All things by immortal power,
Near or far,
Hiddenly
To each other linkèd are,
That thou canst not stir a flower
Without troubling of a star;
When thy song is shield and mirror
To the fair snake-curlèd Pain,
Where thou dar'st affront her terror
That on her thou may'st attain
Perséan conquest; seek no more,
O seek no more!
Pass the gates of Luthany, tread the region Elenore.'

XXIII

So sang she, so wept she,
Through a dream-night's day;
And with her magic singing kept she—
Mystical in music—
That garden of enchanting
In visionary May;
Swayless for my spirit's haunting,
Thrice-threefold walled with emerald from our mortal morn.
    ings grey.

XXIV

And as a necromancer
Raises from the rose-ash
The ghost of the rose;
My heart so made answer
To her voice's silver plash,—
Stirred in reddening flash,
And from out its mortal ruins the purpureal phantom blows.

XXV

Her tears made dulcet fretting,
Her voice had no word,
More than thunder or the bird.
Yet, unforgetting,
The ravished soul her meanings knew. Mine ears heard
    not, and I heard.

XXVI

When she shall unwind
All those wiles she wound about me,
Tears shall break from out me,
That I cannot find
Music in the holy poets to my wistful want, I doubt me!

CONTEMPLATION

THIS morning saw I, fled the shower,
The earth reclining in a lull of power:
The heavens, pursuing not their path,
Lay stretched out naked after bath,
Or so it seemed; field, water, tree, were still,
Nor was there any purpose on the calm-browed hill.

The hill, which sometimes visibly is
Wrought with unresting energies,
Looked idly; from the musing wood,
And every rock, a life renewed
Exhaled like an unconscious thought
When poets, dreaming unperplexed,
Dream that they dream of nought.
Nature one hour appears a thing unsexed,
Or to such serene balance brought
That her twin natures cease their sweet alarms,
And sleep in one another's arms.
The sun with resting pulses seems to brood,
And slacken its command upon my unurged blood.

The river has not any care
Its passionless water to the sea to bear;
The leaves have brown content;
The wall to me has freshness like a scent,
And takes half-animate the air,
Making one life with its green moss and stain;
And life with all things seems too perfect blent
For anything of life to be aware.
The very shades on hill, and tree, and plain,
Where they have fallen doze, and where they doze remain

No hill can idler be than I;
No stone its inter-particled vibration
Investeth with a stiller lie;
No heaven with a more urgent rest betrays
The eyes that on it gaze.
We are too near akin that thou shouldst cheat
Me, Nature, with thy fair deceit.
In poets floating like a water-flower
Upon the bosom of the glassy hour,
In skies that no man sees to move,
Lurk untumultuous vortices of power,
For joy too native, and for agitation
Too instant, too entire for sense thereof,
Motion like gnats when autumn suns are low,
Perpetual as the prisoned feet of love
On the heart's floors with painèd pace that go.
From stones and poets you may know,
Nothing so active is, as that which least seems so.

For he, that conduit running wine of song,
Then to himself does most belong
When he his mortal house unbars
To the importunate and thronging feet
That round our corporal walls unheeded beat;
Till, all containing, he exalt
His stature to the stars, or stars
Narrow their heaven to his fleshly vault:
When like a city under ocean,
To human things he grows a desolation,
And is made a habitation
For the fluctuous universe
To lave with unimpeded motion.
He scarcely frets the atmosphere
With breathing, and his body shares
The immobility of rocks;
His heart's a drop-well of tranquillity;
His mind more still is than the limbs of fear,
And yet its unperturbed velocity
The spirit of the simoom mocks.
He round the solemn centre of his soul
Wheels like a dervish, while his being is
Streamed with the set of the world's harmonies,
In the long draft of whatsoever sphere
He lists the sweet and clear
Clangour of his high orbit on to roll,
So gracious is his heavenly grace;
And the bold stars does hear,
Every one in his airy soar,
For evermore
Shout to each other from the peaks of space,
As 'thwart ravines of azure shouts the mountaineer.

'BY REASON OF THY LAW'

Here I make oath—
Although the heart that knows its bitterness
Hear loath,
And credit less—
That he who kens to meet Pain's kisses fierce
Which hiss against his tears,
Dread, loss, nor love frustrate,
Nor all iniquity of the froward years
Shall his inurèd wing make idly bate,
Nor of the appointed quarry his staunch sight
To lose observance quite;
Seal from half-sad and all-elate
Sagacious eyes
Ultimate Paradise;
Nor shake his certitude of haughty fate.

Pacing the burning shares of many dooms,
I with stern tread do the clear-witting stars
To judgment cite,
If I have borne aright
The proving of their pure-willed ordeal.
From food of all delight
The heavenly Falconer my heart debars,
And tames with fearful glooms
The haggard to His call;
Yet sometimes comes a hand, sometimes a voice withal,
And she sits meek now, and expects the light.
In this Avernian sky,
This sultry and incumbent canopy
Of dull and doomed regret;
Where on the unseen verges yet, O yet,

At intervals,
Trembles, and falls,
Faint lightning of remembered transient sweet—
Ah, far too sweet
But to be sweet a little, a little sweet, and fleet;
Leaving this pallid trace,
This loitering and most fitful light, a space,
Still some sad space,
For Grief to see her own poor face:—
Here where I keep my stand
With all o'er-anguished feet,
And no live comfort near on any hand;
Lo, I proclaim the unavoided term,
When this morass of tears, then drained and firm,
Shall be a land—
Unshaken I affirm—
Where seven-quired psalterings meet;
And all the gods move with calm hand in hand,
And eyes that know not trouble and the worm.

THE DREAD OF HEIGHT

If ye were blind, ye should have no sin: but now ye say:
We see: your sin remaineth. JOHN ix. 41.

Not the Circean wine
Most perilous is for pain:
Grapes of the heavens' star-loaden vine,
Whereto the lofty-placed
Thoughts of fair souls attain,
Tempt with a more retributive delight,
And do disrelish all life's sober taste.

'Tis to have drunk too well
The drink that is divine,
Maketh the kind earth waste,
And breath intolerable.

Ah me!
How shall my mouth content it with mortality?
Lo, secret music, sweetest music,
From distances of distance drifting its lone flight,
Down the arcane where Night would perish in night,
Like a god's loosened locks slips undulously:
Music that is too grievous of the height
For safe and low delight,
Too infinite
For bounded hearts which yet would girth the sea!

So let it be,
Though sweet be great, and though my heart be small:
So let it be,
O music, music, though you wake in me
No joy, no joy at all;
Although you only wake
Uttermost sadness, measure of delight,
Which else I could not credit to the height,
Did I not know,
That ill is statured to its opposite;
Did I not know,
And even of sadness so,
Of utter sadness, make
Of extreme sad a rod to mete
The incredible excess of unsensed sweet,
And mystic wall of strange felicity.
So let it be,

Though sweet be great, and though my heart be small,
And bitter meat
The food of gods for men to eat;
Yea, John ate daintier, and did tread
Less ways of heat,
Than whom to their wind-carpeted
High banquet-hall,
And golden love-feasts, the fair stars entreat.

But ah! withal,
Some hold, some stay,
O difficult Joy, I pray,
Some arms of thine,
Not only, only arms of mine!
Lest like a weary girl I fall
From clasping love so high,
And lacking thus thine arms, then may
Most hapless I
Turn utterly to love of basest rate;
For low they fall whose fall is from the sky.
Yea, who me shall secure
But I, of height grown desperate,
Surcease my wing, and my lost fate
Be dashed from pure
To broken writhings in the shameful slime:
Lower than man, for I dreamed higher,
Thrust down, by how much I aspire,
And damned with drink of immortality?
For such things be,
Yea, and the lowest reach of reeky Hell
Is but made possible
By foreta'en breath of Heaven's austerest clime.

These tidings from the vast to bring
Needeth not doctor nor divine,
Too well, too well
My flesh doth know the heart-perturbing thing;
That dread theology alone
Is mine,
Most native and my own;
And ever with victorious toil
When I have made
Of the deific peaks dim escalade,
My soul with anguish and recoil
Doth like a city in an earthquake rock,
As at my feet the abyss is cloven then,
With deeper menace than for other men,
Of my potential cousinship with mire;
That all my conquered skies do grow a hollow mock,
My fearful powers retire,
No longer strong,
Reversing the shook banners of their song.

Ah, for a heart less native to high Heaven,
A hooded eye, for jesses and restraint,
Or for a will accipitrine to pursue!—
The veil of tutelar flesh to simple livers given,
Or those brave-fledging fervours of the Saint,
Whose heavenly falcon-craft doth never taint,
Nor they in sickest time their ample virtue mew.

ORIENT ODE

Lo, in the sancturaried East,
Day, a dedicated priest
In all his robes pontifical exprest,
Lifteth slowly, lifteth sweetly,
From out its Orient tabernacle drawn,
Yon orbèd sacrament confest
Which sprinkles benediction through the dawn;
And when the grave procession's ceased,
The earth with due illustrious rite
Blessed,—ere the frail fingers featly
Of twilight, violet-cassocked acolyte,
His sacerdotal stoles unvest—
Sets, for high close of the mysterious feast,
The sun in august exposition meetly
Within the flaming monstrance of the West.

O salutaris hostia,
Quœ cœli pandis ostium!
Through breachèd darkness' rampart, a
Divine assaulter, art thou come!
God whom none may live and mark!
Borne within thy radiant ark,
While the Earth, a joyous David,
Dances before thee from the dawn to dark.
The moon, O leave, pale ruined Eve;
Behold her fair and greater daughter*
Offers to thee her fruitful water,
Which at thy first white *Ave* shall conceive!

* The earth.

Thy gazes do on simple her
Desirable allures confer;
What happy comelinesses rise
Beneath thy beautifying eyes!
Who was, indeed, at first a maid
Such as, with sighs, misgives she is not fair,
And secret views herself afraid,
Till flatteries sweet provoke the charms they swear:
Yea, thy gazes, blissful Lover,
Make the beauties they discover!
What dainty guiles and treacheries caught
From artful promptings of love's artless thought
Her lowly loveliness teach her to adorn,
When thy plumes shiver against the conscious gates of morn!

And so the love which is thy dower,
Earth, though her first-frightened breast
Against the exigent boon protest
(For she, poor maid, of her own power
Has nothing in herself, not even love,
But an unwitting void thereof),
Gives back to thee in sanctities of flower;
And holy odours do her bosom invest,
That sweeter grows for being prest:
Though dear recoil, the tremorous nurse of joy,
From thine embrace still startles coy,
Till Phosphor lead, at thy returning hour,
The laughing captive from the wishing West.

Nor the majestic heavens less
Thy formidable sweets approve,
Thy dreads and thy delights confess,
That do draw, and that remove.

Thou as a lion roar'st, O Sun,
Upon thy satellites' vexèd heels;
Before thy terrible hunt thy planets run;
Each in his frighted orbit wheels,
Each flies through inassuageable chase,
Since the hunt o' the world begun,
The puissant approaches of thy face,
And yet thy radiant leash he feels.
Since the hunt o' the world begun,
Lashed with terror, leashed with longing,
The mighty course is ever run;
Pricked with terror, leashed with longing,
Thy rein they love, and thy rebuke they shun.
Since the hunt o' the world began,
With love that trembleth, fear that loveth,
Thou join'st the woman to the man;
And Life with Death
In obscure nuptials moveth,
Commingling alien yet affinèd breath.

Thou art the incarnated Light
Whose Sire is aboriginal, and beyond
Death and resurgence of our day and night;
From him is thy vicegerent wand
With double potence of the black and white.
Giver of Love, and Beauty, and Desire,
The terror, and the loveliness, and purging,
The deathfulness and lifefulness of fire!
Samson's riddling meanings merging
In thy twofold sceptre meet:
Out of thy minatory might,
Burning Lion, burning Lion,
Comes the honey of all sweet,

And out of thee, the Eater, comes forth meat.
And though, by thine alternate breath,
Every kiss thou dost inspire
Echoeth
Back from the windy vaultages of death;
Yet thy clear warranty above
Augurs the wings of death too must
Occult reverberations stir of love
Crescent, and life incredible;
That even the kisses of the just
Go down not unresurgent to the dust.
Yea, not a kiss which I have given,
But shall triumph upon my lips in heaven,
Or cling a shameful fungus there in hell.

Know'st thou me not, O Sun? Yea, well
Thou know'st the ancient miracle,
The children know'st of Zeus and May;
And still thou teachest them, O splendent Brother,
To incarnate, the antique way,
The truth which is their heritage from their Sire
In sweet disguise of flesh from their sweet Mother.
My fingers thou hast taught to con
Thy flame-chorded psalterion,
Till I can translate into mortal wire—
Till I can translate passing well—
The heavenly harping harmony,
Melodious, sealed, inaudible,
Which makes the dulcet psalter of the world's desire.
Thou whisperest in the Moon's white ear,
And she does whisper into mine,—
By night together, I and she—

With her virgin voice divine,
The things I cannot half so sweetly tell
As she can sweetly speak, I sweetly hear.

By her, the Woman, does Earth live, O Lord,
Yet she for Earth, and both in Thee.
Light out of Light!
Resplendent and prevailing Word
Of the Unheard!
Not unto thee, great Image, not to thee
Did the wise heathen bend an idle knee;
And in an age of faith grown frore
If I too shall adore,
Be it accounted unto me
A bright sciential idolatry!
God has given thee visible thunders
To utter thine apocalypse of wonders;
And what want I of prophecy,
That at the sounding from thy station
Of thy flagrant trumpet, see
The seals that melt, the open revelation?
Or who a God-persuading angel needs,
That only heeds
The rhetoric of thy burning deeds?
Which but to sing, if it may be,
In worship-warranting moiety,
So I would win
In such a song as hath within
A smouldering core of mystery,
Brimmèd with nimbler meanings up
Than hasty Gideons in their hands may sup;—
Lo, my suit pleads

That thou, Isaian coal of fire,
Touch from yon altar my poor mouths' desire,
And the relucent song take for thy sacred meeds.

To thine own shape
Thou round'st the chrysolite of the grape,
Bind'st thy gold lightnings in his veins;
Thou storest the white garners of the rains.
Destroyer and preserver, thou
Who medicinest sickness, and to health
Art the unthankèd marrow of its wealth;
To those apparent sovereignties we bow
And bright appurtenances of thy brow!
Thy proper blood dost thou not give,
That Earth, the gusty Mænad, drink and dance?
Art thou not life of them that live?
Yea, in a glad twinkling advent, thou dost dwell
Within our body as a tabernacle!
Thou bittest with thine ordinance
The jaws of Time, and thou dost mete
The unstable treading of his feet.
Thou to thy spousal universe
Art Husband, she thy Wife and Church;
Who in most dusk and vidual curch,
Her Lord being hence,
Keeps her cold sorrows by thy hearse.
The heavens renew their innocence
And morning state
But by thy sacrament communicate;
Their weeping night the symbol of our prayers,
Our darkened search,
And sinful vigil desolate.

Yea biune in imploring dumb,
Essential Heavens and corporal Earth await;
The Spirit and the Bride say: Come!
Lo, of thy Magians I the least
Haste with my gold, my incenses and myrrhs,
To thy desired epiphany, from the spiced
Regions and odorous of Song's traded East.
Thou, for the life of all that live
The victim daily born and sacrificed;
'To whom the pinion of this longing verse
Beats but with fire which first thyself didst give,
To thee, O Sun—or is't perchance to Christ?

Ay, if men say that on all high heaven's face
The saintly signs I trace
Which round my stolèd altars hold their solemn place,
Amen, amen! For oh, how could it be,—
When I with wingèd feet had run
Through all the windy earth about,
Quested its secret of the sun,
And heard what things the stars together shout,—
I should not heed thereout
Consenting counsel won:—
'By this, O Singer, know we if thou see.
When men shall say to thee: Lo! Christ is here,
When men shall say to thee: Lo! Christ is there,
Believe them: yea, and this—then art thou seer,
When all thy crying clear
Is but: Lo here! lo there!—ah me, lo everywhere!'

NEW YEAR'S CHIMES

WHAT is the song the stars sing?
  (*And a million songs are as song of one*)
This is the song the stars sing:
  (*Sweeter song's none*)

One to set, and many to sing,
  (*And a million songs are as song*
One to stand, and many to cling,
The many things, and the one Thing,
  The one that runs not, the many that **run.**

The ever new weaveth the ever old,
  (*And a million songs are as song of one*)
Ever telling the never told;
The silver saith, and the saith is gold,
  And done ever the never done.

The Chase that's chased is the Lord o' the **chase,**
  (*And a million songs are as song of one*)
And the Pursued cries on the race;
  And the hounds in leash are the hounds that **run.**

Hidden stars by the shown stars' sheen;
  (*And a million suns are but as one*)
Colours unseen by the colours seen,
And sounds unheard heard sounds between,
  And a night is in the light of the sun.

An ambuscade of light in night,
   (*And a million secrets are but as one*)
And a night is dark in the sun's light,
   And a world in the world man looks upon.

Hidden stars by the shown stars' wings,
   (*And a million cycles are but as one*)
And a world with unapparent strings
Knits the simulant world of things;
   Behold, and vision thereof is none.

The world above in the world below,
   (*And a million worlds are but as one*)
And the One in all; as the sun's strength so
Strives in all strength, glows in all glow
   Of the earth that wits not, and man thereon.

Braced in its own fourfold embrace
   (*And a million strengths are as strength of one*)
And round it all God's arms of grace,
The world, so as the Vision says,
   Doth with great lightning-tramples run.

And thunder bruiteth into thunder,
   (*And a million sounds are as sound of one*)
From stellate peak to peak is tossed a voice of wonder,
And the height stoops down to the depths thereunder,
   And sun leans forth to his brother-sun.

And the more ample years unfold
   (*With a million songs as song of one*)
A little new of the ever old,
A little told of the never told,
   Added act of the never done.

Loud the descant, and low the theme,
   (*A million songs are as song of one*)
And the dream of the world is dream in dream,
But the one Is is, or nought could seem;
   And the song runs round to the song begun.

This is the song the stars sing,
   (*Toned all in time*)
Tintinnabulous, tuned to ring
A multitudinous-single thing
   (*Rung all in rhyme*).

FROM THE NIGHT OF FOREBEING

AN ODE AFTER EASTER

In the chaos of preordination, and night of our forebeings.
                     SIR THOMAS BROWNE.
Et lux in tenebris erat, et tenebræ eam non comprehenderunt.
                     ST. JOHN.

CAST wide the folding doorways of the East,
For now is light increased!
And the wind-besomed chambers of the air,
See they be garnished fair;

And look the ways exhale some precious odours,
And set ye all about wild-breathing spice,
Most fit for Paradise!
Now is no time for sober gravity,
Season enough has Nature to be wise;
But now disinct, with raiment glittering free,
Shake she the ringing rafters of the skies
With festal footing and bold joyance sweet,
And let the earth be drunken and carouse!
For lo, into her house
Spring is come home with her world-wandering feet,
And all things are made young with young desires;
And all for her is light increased
In yellow stars and yellow daffodils,
And East to West, and West to East,
Fling answering welcome-fires,
By dawn and day-fall, on the jocund hills.
And ye, winged minstrels of her fair meinie,
Being newly coated in glad livery,
Upon her steps attend,
And round her treading dance, and without end
Reel your shrill lutany.
What popular breath her coming does out-tell
The garrulous leaves among!
What little noises stir and pass
From blade to blade along the voluble grass!
O Nature, never-done
Ungaped-at Pentecostal miracle,
We hear thee, each man in his proper tongue!
Break, elemental children, break ye loose
From the strict frosty rule
Of grey-beard Winter's school.

Vault, O young winds, vault in your tricksome courses
Upon the snowy steeds that reinless use
In cœrule pampas of the heaven to run;
Foaled of the white sea-horses,
Washed in the lambent waters of the sun.
Let even the slug-abed snail upon the thorn
Put forth a conscious horn!
Mine elemental co-mates, joy each one;
And ah, my foster-brethren, seem not sad—
No, seem not sad,
That my strange heart and I should be so little glad.
Suffer me at your leafy feast
To sit apart, a somewhat alien guest,
And watch your mirth,
Unsharing in the liberal laugh of earth;
Yet with a sympathy
Begot of wholly sad and half-sweet memory—
The little sweetness making grief complete;
Faint wind of wings from hours that distant beat,
When I, I too,
Was once, O wild companions, as are you,—
Ran with such wilful feet;
Wraith of a recent day and dead,
Risen wanly overhead,
Frail, strengthless as a noon-belated moon,
Or as the glazing eyes of watery heaven,
When the sick night sinks into deathly swoon.

A higher and a solemn voice
I heard through your gay-hearted noise;
A solemn meaning and a stiller voice
Sounds to me from far days when I too shall rejoice,

Nor more be with your jollity at strife.
O prophecy
Of things that are, and are not, and shall be!
The great-vanned Angel March
Hath trumpeted
His clangorous 'Sleep no more' to all the dead—
Beat his strong vans o'er earth, and air, and sea.
And they have heard;
Hark to the *Jubilate* of the bird
For them that found the dying way to life!
And they have heard,
And quicken to the great precursive word;
Green spray showers lightly down the cascade of the larch;
The graves are riven,
And the Sun cames with power amid the clouds of heaven!
Before his way
Went forth the trumpet of the March;
Before his way, before his way
Dances the pennon of the May!
O Earth, unchilded, widowed Earth, so long
Lifting in patient pine and ivy-tree
Mournful belief and steadfast prophecy,
Behold how all things are made true!
Behold your bridegroom cometh in to you,
Exceeding glad and strong.
Raise up your eyes, O raise your eyes abroad!
No more shall you sit sole and vidual,
Searching, in servile pall,
Upon the hieratic night the star-sealed sense of all:
Rejoice, O barren, and look forth abroad!
Your children gathered back to your embrace
See with a mother's face;

Look up, O mortals, and the portent heed!
In very deed,
Washed with new fire to their irradiant birth,
Reintegrated are the heavens and earth;
From sky to sod,
The world's unfolded blossom smells of God.

O imagery
Of that which was the first, and is the last!
For, as the dark profound nativity,
God saw the end should be,
When the world's infant horoscope He cast.
Unshackled from the bright Phœbean awe,
In leaf, flower, mold, and tree,
Resolved into individual liberty,
Most strengthless, unparticipant, inane,
Or suffered the ill peace of lethargy,
Lo, the Earth eased of rule:
Unsummered, granted to her own worst smart
The dear wish of the fool—
Disintegration, merely which man's heart
For freedom understands,
Amid the frog-like errors from the damp
And quaking swamp
Of the low popular levels spawned in all the lands.
But thou, O Earth, dost much disdain
The bondage of thy waste and futile reign,
And sweetly to the great compulsion draw
Of God's alone true-manumitting law,
And Freedom, only which the wise intend,
To work thine innate end.
Over thy vacant counterfeit of death

Broods with soft urgent breath
Love, that is child of Beauty and of Awe:
To intercleavage of sharp warring pain,
As of contending chaos come again,
Thou wak'st, O Earth,
And work'st from change to change and birth to birth
Creation old as hope, and new as sight;
For meed of toil not vain,
Hearing once more the primal fiat toll:
'Let there be light!'
And there is light!
Light fragrant, manifest,
Light to the zenith, light from pole to pole,
Light from the East that waxeth to the West,
And with its puissant goings-forth
Encroaches on the South and on the North;
And with its great approaches does prevail
Upon the sullen fastness of the height,
And summoning its levied power
Crescent and confident through the crescent hour,
Goes down with laughters on the subject vale:
Light flagrant, manifest,
Light to the sentient closeness of the breast,
Light to the secret chambers of the brain!
And thou up-floatest, warm, and newly-bathed,
Earth, through delicious air,
And with thine own apparent beauties swathed,
Wringing the waters from thine arborous hair;
That all men's hearts, which do behold and see
Grow weak with their exceeding much desire,
And turn to thee on fire,
Enamoured with their utter wish of thee,

Anadyomene!
What vine-outquickening life all creatures sup,
Feel, for the air within its sapphire cup
How it does leap, and twinkle headily!
Feel, for Earth's bosom pants, and heaves her scarfing sea;
And round and round in bacchanal rout reel the swift spheres
    intemperably!
My little-worlded self! the shadows pass
In this thy sister-world, as in a glass,
Of all processions that revolve in thee:
Not only of cyclic Man
Thou here discern'st the plan,
Not only of cyclic Man, but of the cyclic Me.
Not solely of Mortality's great years
The reflex just appears,
But thine own bosom's year, still circling round
In ample and in ampler gyre
Toward the far completion, wherewith crowned
Love unconsumed shall chant in his own furnace-fire.
How many trampled and deciduous joys
Enrich thy soul for joys deciduous still,
Before the distance shall fulfil
Cyclic unrest with solemn equipoise!
Happiness is the shadow of things past,
Which fools still take for that which is to be!
And not all foolishly:
For all the past, read true, is prophecy,
And all the firsts are hauntings of some Last,
And all the springs are flash-lights of one Spring.
Then leaf, and flower, and fall-less fruit
Shall hang together on the unyellowing bough;
And silence shall be Music mute

For her surchargèd heart. Hush thou!
These things are far too sure that thou should'st **dream**
Thereof, lest they appear as things that seem.

Shade within shade! for deeper in the glass
Now other imaged meanings pass;
And as the man, the poet there is read.
Winter with me, alack!
Winter on every hand I find:
Soul, brain, and pulses dead,
The mind no further by the warm sense fed,
The soul weak-stirring in the arid mind,
More tearless-weak to flash itself abroad
Than the earth's life beneath the frost-scorched sod.
My lips have drought, and crack,
By laving music long unvisited.
Beneath the austere and macerating rime
Draws back constricted in its icy urns
The genial flame of Earth, and there
With torment and with tension does prepare
The lush disclosures of the vernal time.
All joys draw inward to their icy urns,
Tormented by constraining rime,
And there
With undelight and throe prepare
The bounteous efflux of the vernal time.
Nor less beneath compulsive Law
Rebukèd draw
The numbèd musics back upon my heart;
Whose yet-triumphant course I know
And prevalent pulses forth shall start.
Like cataracts that with thunderous hoof charge the disband-
ing snow.

All power is bound
In quickening refusal so;
And silence is the lair of sound;
In act its impulse to deliver,
With fluctuance and quiver
The endeavouring thew grows rigid. Strong
From its retracted coil strikes the resilient song.

Giver of spring,
And song, and every young new thing!
Thou only seest in me, so stripped and bare,
The lyric secret waiting to be born,
The patient term allowed
Before it stretch and flutteringly unfold
Its rumpled webs of amethyst-freaked, diaphanous gold.
And what hard task abstracts me from delight,
Filling with hopeless hope and dear despair
The still-born day and parchèd fields of night,
That my old way of song, no longer fair,
For lack of serene care,
Is grown a stony and a weed-choked plot,
Thou only know'st aright,
Thou only know'st, for I know not.
How many songs must die that this may live!
And shall this most rash hope and fugitive,
Fulfilled with beauty and with might
In days whose feet are rumorous on the air,
Make me forget to grieve
For songs which might have been, nor ever were?
Stern the denial, the travail slow,
The struggling wall will scantly grow:

And though with that dread rite of sacrifice
Ordained for during edifice,
How long, how long ago!
Into that wall which will not thrive
I build myself alive,
Ah, who shall tell me will the wall uprise?
Thou wilt not tell me, who dost only know!
Yet still in mind I keep,
He that observes the wind shall hardly sow,
He that regards the clouds shall hardly reap.
Thine ancient way! I give,
Nor wit if I receive;
Risk all, who all would gain; and blindly. Be it so.

'And blindly,' said I?—No!
That saying I unsay: the wings
Hear I not in prævenient winnowings
Of coming songs, that lift my hair and stir it?
What winds with music wet do the sweet storm foreshow!
Utter stagnation
Is the solstitial slumber of the spirit,
The blear and blank negation of all life:
But these sharp questionings mean strife, and strife
Is the negation of negation.
The thing from which I turn my troubled look,
Fearing the god's rebuke;
That perturbation putting glory on,
As is the golden vortex in the West
Over the foundered sun;
That—but low breathe it, lest the Nemesis
Unchild me, vaunting this—
Is bliss, the hid, hugged, swaddled bliss!

O youngling Joy carest!
That on my now first-mothered breast
Pliest the strange wonder of thine infant lip,
What this aghast surprise of keenest panging,
Wherefrom I blench, and cry thy soft mouth rest?
Ah hold, withhold, and let the sweet mouth slip!
So, with such pain, recoils the woolly dam,
Unused, affrighted, from her yeanling lamb:
I, one with her in cruel fellowship,
Marvel what unmaternal thing I am.

Nature enough! Within thy glass
Too many and too stern the shadows pass.
In this delighted season, flaming
For thy resurrection-feast,
Ah, more I think the long ensepulture cold,
Than stony winter rolled
From the unsealed mouth of the holy East;
The snowdrop's saintly stoles less heed
Than the snow-cloistered penance of the seed.
'Tis the weak flesh reclaiming
Against the ordinance
Which yet for just the accepting spirit scans.
Earth waits, and patient heaven,
Self-bonded God doth wait
Thrice-promulgated bans
Of his fair nuptial-date.
And power is man's,
With that great word of 'Wait,'
To still the sea of tears,
And shake the iron heart of Fate.
In that one word is strong

And else, alas, much-mortal song;
With sight to pass the frontier of all spheres,
And voice which does my sight such wrong.

Not without fortitude I wait
The dark majestical ensuit
Of destiny, nor peevish rate
Calm-knowledged Fate.
I, that no part have in the time's bragged way,
And its loud bruit;
I, in this house so rifted, marred,
So ill to live in, hard to leave;
I, so star-weary, over-warred,
That have no joy in this your day—
Rather foul fume englutting, that of day
Confounds all ray—
But only stand aside and grieve;
I yet have sight beyond the smoke,
And kiss the gods' feet, though they wreak
Upon me stroke and again stroke;
And this my seeing is not weak.
The Woman I behold, whose vision seek
All eyes and know not; t'ward whom climb
The steps o' the world, and beats all wing of rhyme,
And knows not; 'twixt the sun and moon
Her inexpressible front enstarred
Tempers the wrangling spheres to tune;
Their divergent harmonies
Concluded in the concord of her eyes,
And vestal dances of her glad regard.
I see, which fretteth with surmise
Much heads grown unsagacious-grey,

The slow aim of wise-hearted Time,
Which folded cycles within cycles cloak:
We pass, we pass, we pass; this does not pass away,
But holds the furrowing earth still harnessed to its yoke.
The stars still write their golden purposes
On heaven's high palimpsest, and no man sees,
Nor any therein Daniel; I do hear
From the revolving year
A voice which cries:
'All dies;
Lo, how all dies! O seer,
And all things too arise:
All dies, and all is born;
But each resurgent morn, behold, more near the Perfect
    Morn.'

Firm is the man, and set beyond the cast
Of Fortune's game, and the iniquitous hour,
Whose falcon soul sits fast,
And not intends her high sagacious tour
Or ere the quarry sighted; who looks past
To slow much sweet from little instant sour,
And in the first does always see the last.

ANY SAINT

His shoulder did I hold
Too high that I, o'erbold
    Weak one,
    Should lean thereon.

But He a little hath
Declined His stately path
  And my
  Feet set more high;

That the slack arm may reach
His shoulder, and faint speech
  Stir
  His unwithering hair.

And bolder now and bolder
I lean upon that shoulder,
  So dear
  He is and near:

And with His aureole
The tresses of my soul
  Are blent
  In wished content.

Yea, this too gentle Lover
Hath flattering words to move her
  To pride
  By His sweet side.

Ah, Love! somewhat let be—
Lest my humility
  Grow weak
  When Thou dost speak.

Rebate Thy tender suit,
Lest to herself impute
  Some worth
  Thy bride of earth!

A maid too easily
Conceits herself to be
          Those things
     Her lover sings;

And being straitly wooed,
Believes herself the Good
          And Fair
     He seeks in her.

Turn something of Thy look,
And fear me with rebuke,
          That I
     May timorously

Take tremors in Thy arms,
And with contrivèd charms
          Allure
     A love unsure.

Not to me, not to me,
Builded so flawfully,
          O God,
     Thy humbling laud!

Not to this man, but Man,—
Universe in a span;
          Point
     Of the spheres conjoint;

In whom eternally
Thou, Light, dost focus Thee!—
          Didst pave
          The way o' the wave;

Rivet with stars the Heaven,
For causeways to Thy driven
          Car
          In its coming far

Unto him, only him;
In Thy deific whim
          Didst bound
          Thy works' great round

In this small ring of flesh;
The sky's gold-knotted mesh
          Thy wrist
          Did only twist

To take him in that net.—
Man! swinging-wicket set
          Between
          The Unseen and Seen;

Lo, God's two worlds immense,
Of spirit and of sense,
          Wed
          In this narrow bed;

Yea, and the midge's hymn
Answers the seraphim
          Athwart
          Thy body's court!

Great arm-fellow of God!
To the ancestral clod
        Kin,
        And to cherubin;

Bread predilectedly
O' the worm and Deity!
        Hark,
        O God's clay-sealed Ark,

To praise that fits thee, clear
To the ear within the ear,
        But dense
        To clay-sealed sense.

All the Omnific made
When, in a word he said,
        (Mystery!)
        He uttered *thee;*

Thee His great utterance bore,
O secret metaphor
        Of what
        Thou dream'st no jot!

Cosmic metonymy;
Weak world-unshuttering key;
        One
        Seal of Solomon!

Trope that itself not scans
Its huge significance,
      Which tries
    Cherubic eyes!

Primer where the angels all
God's grammar spell in small,
      Nor spell
    The highest too well!

Point for the great descants
Of starry disputants:
      Equation
    Of creation!

Thou meaning, couldst thou see,
Of all which dafteth thee;
      So plain,
    It mocks thy pain.

Stone of the Law indeed,
Thine own self couldst thou read;
      Thy bliss
    Within thee is.

Compost of Heaven and mire,
Slow foot and swift desire!
      Lo,
    To have Yes, choose No;

Gird, and thou shalt unbind;
Seek not, and thou shalt find;
    To eat,
      Deny thy meat;

And thou shalt be fulfilled
With all sweet things unwilled:
    So best
      God loves to jest

With children small—a freak
Of heavenly hide-and-seek
    Fit
      For thy wayward wit.

Who are thyself a thing
Of whim and wavering;
    Free
      When His wings pen thee;

Sole fully blest, to feel
God whistle thee at heel;
    Drunk up
      As a dew-drop,

When He bends down, sun-wise,
Intemperable eyes;
    Most proud,
      When utterly bowed,

To feel thyself and be
His dear nonentity—
  Caught
  Beyond human thought

In the thunder-spout of Him,
Until thy being dim,
  And be
  Dead deathlessly.

Stoop, stoop; for thou dost fear
The nettle's wrathful spear,
  So slight
  Art thou of might!

Rise; for Heaven hath no frown
When thou to thee pluck'st down,
  Strong clod!
  The neck of God.

ASSUMPTA MARIA

Thou needst not make new songs, but say the old.
       —COWLEY.

'Mortals, that behold a Woman
  Rising 'twixt the Moon and Sun;
Who am I the heavens assume? an
All am I, and I am one.

'Multitudinous ascend I,
   Dreadful as a battle arrayed,
For I bear you whither tend I;
   Ye are I: be undismayed!
I, the Ark that for the graven
   Tables of the Law was made;
Man's own heart was one; one, Heaven;
   Both within my womb were laid.
     For there Anteros with Eros,
       Heaven with man, conjoinèd was,—
     Twin-stone of the Law, *Ischyros,*
       Agios Athanatos.

'I, the flesh-girt Paradises
   Gardenered by the Adam new,
Daintied o'er with dear devices
   Which He loved, for He grew.
I, the boundless strict Savannah
   Which God's leaping feet go through;
I, the Heaven whence the Manna,
   Weary Israel, slid on you!
     He the Anteros and Eros,
       I the body, He the Cross;
     He upbeareth me, *Ischyros,*
       Agios Athanatos!

'I am Daniel's mystic Mountain,
   Whence the mighty stone was rolled;
I am the four Rivers' Fountain,
   Watering Paradise of old;
Cloud down-raining the Just One am,
   Danae of the Shower of Gold;

I the Hostel of the Sun am;
 He the Lamb, and I the Fold.
  He the Anteros and Eros,
   I the body, He the Cross;
  He is fast to me, *Ischyros,*
   Agios Athanatos!

'I, the Presence-hall where Angels
 Do enwheel their placèd King—
Even my thoughts which, without change else,
 Cyclic burn and cyclic sing.
To the hollow of Heaven transplanted,
 I a breathing Eden spring,
Where with venom all outpanted
 Lies the slimed Curse shrivelling.
  For the brazen Serpent clear on
   That old fangèd knowledge shone;
  I to Wisdom rise, *Ischyron,*
   Agion Athanaton!

'Then commanded and spake to me
 He who framed all things that be;
And my Maker entered through me,
 In my tent His rest took He.
Lo! He standeth, Spouse and Brother,
 I to Him, and He to me,
Who upraised me where my mother
 Fell, beneath the apple-tree.
  Risen 'twixt Anteros and Eros,
   Blood and Water, Moon and Sun,
  He upbears me, He *Ischyros,*
   I bear Him, the *Athanaton!*'

Where is laid the Lord arisen?
   In the light we walk in gloom;
Though the Sun has burst his prison,
   We know not his biding-room.
Tell us where the Lord sojourneth,
   For we find an empty tomb.
Whence He sprung, there He returneth,
   Mystic Sun,—the Virgin's Womb.'
      Hidden Sun, His beams so near us,
         Cloud-enpillared as He was
      From of old, there He, *Ischyros*,
         Waits our search, *Athanatos*.

Who is She, in candid vesture,
   Rushing up from out the brine?
Treading with resilient gesture
   Air, and with that Cup divine?
She in us and we in her are,
   Beating Godward: all that pine,
Lo, a wonder and a terror—
   The Sun hath blushed the Sea to Wine!
      He the Anteros and Eros,
         She the Bride and Spirit; for
      Now the days of promise near us,
         And the Sea shall be no more.

Open wide thy gates, O Virgin,
   That the King may enter thee!
At all gates the clangours gurge in,
   God's paludament lightens, see!
Camp of Angels! Well we even
 , Of this thing may doubtful be,—

If thou art assumed to Heaven,
  Or is Heaven assumed to thee!
    Consummatum. Christ the promised,
      Thy maiden realm, is won, O Strong!
      Since to such sweet Kingdom comest,
        Remember me, poor Thief of Song!

Cadent fails the stars along:—
  Mortals, that behold a woman
    Rising 'twixt the Moon and Sun;
  Who am I the heavens assume? an
    All am I, and I am one.

CARMEN GENESIS

I

Sing how the uncreated Light
Moved first upon the deep and night,
  And, at Its *fiat lux*,
Created light unfurled, to be
God's pinions—stirred perpetually
  In flux and in reflux.

From light create, and the vexed ooze,
God shaped to potency and thews
  All things we see, and all
Which lessen, beyond human mark,
Into the spaces Man calls dark
  Because his day is small.

Far-storied, lanterned with the skies,
All Nature, magic-palace-wise,
   Did from the waters come:
The angelic singing-masons knew
How many centuried centuries through
   The awful courses clomb.

The regent light his strong decree
Then laid upon the snarling sea;
   Shook all its wallowing girth
The shaggy brute, and did (for wrath
Low bellowing in its chafèd path)
   Sullen disglut the Earth.

Meanwhile the universal light
Broke itself into bounds; and Night
   And Day were two, yet one:
Dividual splendour did begin
Its procreant task, and, globing, spin
   In moon, and stars, and sun.

With interspheral counterdance
Consenting contraries advance,
   And plan is hid for plan:
In roaring harmonies would burst
The thunder's throat; the heavens, uncurst,
   Restlessly steady ran.

All day Earth waded in the sun,
Free-bosomed; and, when Night begun,
   Spelt in the secret stars.

Day unto Day did utter speech,
Night unto Night the knowledge teach
   Barred in its golden bars.

And, last, Man's self, the little world
Where was Creation's semblance furled,
   Rose at the linking nod:
For the first world, the moon and sun
Swung orbed. That human second one
   Was dark, and waited God.

His locks He spread upon the breeze,
His feet He lifted on the seas,
   Into His worlds He came:
Man made confession: 'There is Light!'
And named, while Nature to its height
   Quailed, the enormous Name.

II

Poet! still, still thou dost rehearse,
In the great *fiat* of thy Verse,
   Creation's primal plot;
And what thy Maker in the whole
Worked, little maker, in thy soul
   Thou work'st, and men know not.

Thine intellect, a luminous voice,
Compulsive moved above the noise
   Of thy still-fluctuous sense;
And Song, a water-child like Earth,
Stands with feet sea-washed, a wild birth
   Amid their subsidence.

Bold copyist! who dost relimn
The traits, in man's gross mind grown **dim**,
  Of the first Masterpiece—
Re-marking all in thy one Day:—
God give thee Sabbath to repay
  Thy sad work with full peace!

Still Nature, to the clang of doom,
Thy Verse rebeareth in her womb;
  Thou makest all things new,
Elias, when thou comest! yea,
Mak'st straight the intelligential way
  For God to pace into.

His locks perturb man's eddying thought,
His feet man's surgy breast have sought,
  To man, His World, He came;
Man makes confession: 'There is light!'
And names, while Being to its height
  Rocks, the desirèd Name..

III

God! if not yet the royal siege
Of Thee, my terrible sweet Liege,
  Hath shook my soul to fall;
If, 'gainst Thy great investment, **still**
Some broken bands of rebel Will
  Do man the desperate wall;

Yet, yet, Thy graciousness! I tread,
All quick, through tribes of moving dead—
  Whose life's a sepulchre
Sealed with the dull stone of a heart
No angel can roll round. I start,
  Thy sercets lie so bare!

With beautiful importunacy
All things plead, 'We are fair!' To me
  Thy world's a morning haunt,
A bride whose zone no man hath slipt
But I, with baptism still bedript
  Of the prime water's font.

AD CASTITATEM

THROUGH thee, Virginity, endure
The stars, most integral and pure,
    And ever contemplate
    Themselves inviolate

In waters, and do love unknown
Beauty they dream not is their own!
    Through thee the waters bare
    Their bossoms to the air,

And with confession never done
Admit the sacerdotal sun,
    Absolved eternally
    By his asperging eye.

To tread the floor of lofty souls,
With thee Love mingles aureoles;
    Who walk his mountain-peak
    Thy sister-hand must seek.

A hymen all unguessed of men
In dreams thou givest to my ken;
    For lacking of like mate,
    Eternally frustrate:

Where, that the soul of either spouse
Securelier clasp in either's house,
    They never breach at all
    Their walls corporeal.

This was the secret of the great
And primal Paradisal state,
    Which Adam and which Eve
    Might not again retrieve.

Yet hast thou toward my vision **taught**
A way to draw in vernal thought,
    Not all too far from that
    Great Paradisal state,

Which for that earthy men might **wrong**,
Were't uttered in this earthless song,
    Thou layest cold finger-tips
    Upon my histed lips.

But thou, who knowest the hidden thing
Thou hast instructed me to sing,
    Teach Love the way to be
    A new Virginity!

Do thou with thy protecting hand
Shelter the flame thy breath has fanned;
    Let my heart's reddest glow
    Be but as sun-flushed snow.

And if they say that snow is cold,
O Chastity, must they be told
    The hand that's chafed with snow
    Takes a redoubled glow?—

That extreme cold like heat doth sear?
O to this heart of love draw near,
    And feel how scorching rise
    Its white-cold purities!

Life, ancient and o'er-childed nurse,
To turn my thirsting mouth averse,
    Her breast embittereth
    With wry foretaste of death:

But thou, sweet Lady Chastity,
Thou, and thy brother Love with thee,
    Upon her lap may'st still
    Sustain me, if thou will.

Out of the terrors of the tomb,
And unclean shapes that haunt sleep's gloom,
    Yet, yet I call on thee,—
      'Abandon thou not me!'

Now sung is all the singing of this chant.
Lord, Lord, be nigh unto me in my want!
For to the idols of the Gentiles I
Will never make me an hierophant:—
Their false-fair gods of gold and ivory,
Which have a mouth, nor any speech thereby,
Save such as soundeth from the throat of hell
The aboriginal lie;
And eyes, nor any seeing in the light,—
Gods of the obscene night,
To whom the darkness is for diadem.
Let them that serve them be made like to them,
Yea, like to him who fell
Shattered in Gaza, as the Hebrews tell,
Before the simple presence of the Ark.

My singing is gone out upon the dark.

THE AFTER WOMAN

DAUGHTER of the ancient Eve,
We know the gifts ye gave—and give.
Who knows the gifts which *you* shall give,
Daughter of the newer Eve?
You, if my soul be augur, you
Shall—O what shall you not, Sweet, do?

The celestial traitress play,
And all mankind to bliss betray;
With sacrosanct cajoleries
And starry treachery of your eyes,
Tempt us back to Paradise!
Make heavenly trespass;—ay, press in
Where faint the fledge-foot seraphin,
Blest fool! Be ensign of our wars,
And shame us all to warriors!
Unbanner your bright locks,—advance,
Gird, their gilded puissance
I' the mystic vaward, and draw on
After the lovely gonfalon
Us to out-folly the excess
Of your sweet foolhardiness;
To adventure like intense
Assault against Omnipotence!

Give me song, as She is, new,
Earth should turn in time thereto!
New, and new, and thrice so new,
All old sweets, New Sweet, meant you!
Fair, I had a dream of thee,
When my young heart beat prophecy,
And in apparition elate
Thy little breasts knew waxèd great,
Sister of the Canticle,
And thee for God grown marriageable.

How my desire desired your day,
That, wheeled in rumour on its way,
Shook me thus with presentience! Then
Eden's lopped tree shall shoot again:

For who Christ's eyes shall miss, with those
Eyes for evident nuncios?
Or who be tardy to His call
In your accents augural?
Who shall not feel the Heavens hid
Impend, at tremble of your lid,
And divine advent shine avowed
Under that dim and lucid cloud;
Yea, 'fore the silver apocalypse,
Fail, at the unsealing of your lips?
When to love *you* is (O Christ's Spouse!)
To love the beauty of His house;
Then come the Isaian days; the old
Shall dream; and our young men behold
Vision—yea, the vision of Thabor-mount,
Which none to other shall recount,
Because in all men's hearts shall be
The seeing and the prophecy.
For ended is the Mystery Play,
When Christ is life, and you the way;
When Egypt's spoils are Israel's right,
And Day fulfils the married arms of Night.
But here my lips are still.
Until
You and the hour shall be revealed,
This song is sung and sung not, and its words are
    sealed.

GRACE OF THE WAY

'My brother!' spake she to the sun;
  The kindred kisses of the stars
Were hers; her feet were set upon
  The moon.   If slumber solved the bars

Of sense, or sense transpicuous grown
  Fulfillèd seeing unto sight,
I know not; nor if 'twas my own
  Ingathered self that made her night.

The windy trammel of her dress,
  Her blown locks, took my soul in mesh;
God's breath they spake, with visibleness
  That stirred the raiment of her flesh:

And sensible, as her blown locks were,
  Beyond the precincts of her form
I felt the woman flow from her—
  A calm of intempestuous storm.

I failed against the affluent tide;
  Out of this abject earth of me
I was translated and enskied
  Into the heavenly-regioned She.

Now of that vision I bereaven
  This knowledge keep, that may not dim:—
Short arm needs man to reach to Heaven,
  So ready is Heaven to stoop to him;

Which sets, to measure of man's feet,
  No alien Tree for trysting-place;
And who can read, may read the sweet
  Direction in his Lady's face.

And pass and pass the daily crowd,
  Unwares, occulted Paradise;
Love the lost plot cries silver-loud,
  Nor any know the tongue he cries.

The light is in the darkness, and
  The darkness doth not comprehend:
God hath no haste; and God's sons stand
  Yet a day, tarrying for the end.

Dishonoured Rahab still hath hid,
  Yea still, within her house of shame,
The messengers by Jesus bid
  Forerun the coming of His Name.

The Word was flesh, and crucified,
  From the beginning, and blasphemed:
Its profaned raiment men divide,
  Damned by what, reverenced, had redeemed.

Thy Lady, was thy heart not blind,
  One hour gave to thy witless trust
The key thou go'st about to find;
  And thou hast dropped it in the dust.

Of her, the Way's one mortal grace,
  Own, save thy seeing be all forgot,
That, truly, God was in this place,
  And thou, unblessèd, knew'st it not.

But some have eyes, and will not see;
  And some would see, and have not eyes;
And fail the tryst, yet find the Tree,
  And take the lesson for the prize.

RETROSPECT

ALAS, and I have sung
Much song of matters vain,
And a heaven-sweetened tongue
Turned to unprofiting strain
Of vacant things, which though
Even so they be, and thoroughly so,
It is no boot at all for thee to know,
But babble and false pain.

What profit if the sun
Put forth his radiant thews,
And on his circuit run,
Even after my device, to this and to that use;
And the true Orient, Christ,
Make not His cloud of thee?
I have sung vanity,
And nothing well devised.

And though the cry of stars
Give tongue before His way
Goldenly, as I say,
And each from wide Saturnus to hot Mars
He calleth by its name,
Lest that its bright feet stray;
And thou have lore of all,
But to thine own Sun's call
Thy path disorbed hast never wit to tame;
It profits not withal,
And my rede is but lame.
Only that, 'mid vain vaunt
Of wisdom ignorant,
A little kiss upon the feet of Love
My hasty verse has stayed
Sometimes a space to plant;
It has not wholly strayed,
Not wholly missed near sweet, fanning proud
        plumes above.

Therefore I do repent
That with religion vain,
And misconceivèd pain,
I have my music bent
To waste on bootless things its skiey-gendered rain:
Yet shall a wiser day
Fulfil more heavenly way
And with approvèd music clear this slip,
I trust in God most sweet.
Meantime the silent lip,
Meantime the climbing feet.

A NARROW VESSEL

BEING A LITTLE DRAMATIC SEQUENCE ON THE ASPECT OF PRIMITIVE GIRL-NATURE TOWARDS A LOVE BEYOND ITS CAPACITIES

A GIRL'S SIN

I.—IN HER EYES

Cross child! red, and frowning so?
    'I, the day just over,
Gave a lock of hair to—no!
    How *dare* you say, my lover?'

He asked you?—Let me understand;
    Come, child, let me sound it!
'Of course, he *would* have asked it, and—
    And so—somehow—he—found it.

'He told it out with great loud eyes—
    Men have such little wit!
His sin I ever will chastise
    Because I gave him it.

'Shameless in me the gift, alas!
    In him his open bliss:
But for the privilege he has
    A thousand he shall miss!

240

'His eyes, where once I dreadless laughed,
    Call up a burning blot:
I hate him, for his shameful craft
    That asked by asking not!'

Luckless boy! and all for hair
    He never asked, you said?
'Not just—but then he gazed—I swear
    He gazed it from my head!

'His silence on my cheek like breath
    I felt in subtle way;
More sweet than aught another saith
    Was what he did not say.

'He'll think me vanquished, for this lapse,
    Who should be above him;
Perhaps he'll think me light; perhaps—
    Perhaps he'll think I—love him!

'Are his eyes conscious and elate,
    I hate him that I blush;
Or are they innocent, still I hate—
    They mean a thing's to hush.

'Before he naught amiss could do,
    Now all things show amiss;
'Twas all my fault, I know that true,
    But all my fault was his.

'I hate him for his mute distress,
   'Tis insult he should care!
Because my heart's all humbleness,
   All pride is in my air.

'With him, each favour that I do
   Is bold suit's hallowing text;
Each gift a bastion levelled to
   The next one and the next.

'Each wish whose grant may him befall
   Is clogged by those withstood;
He trembles, hoping one means all,
   And I, lest perhaps it should.

'Behind me piecemeal gifts I cast,
   My fleeing self to save;
And that's the thing must go at last,
   For that's the thing he'd have.

'My lock the enforcèd steel did grate
   To cut; its root-thrills came
Down to my bosom. It might sate
   His lust for my poor shame!

'His sifted dainty this should be
   For a score ambrosial years!
But his too much humility
   Alarums me with fears.

'My gracious grace a breach he counts
  For graceless escalade;
And, though he's silent ere he mounts,
  My watch is not betrayed.

'My heart hides from my soul he's sweet:
  Ah dread, if he divine!
One touch, I might fall at his feet,
  And he might rise from mine.

'To hear him praise my eyes' brown gleams
  Was native, safe delight;
But now it usurpation seems,
  Because I've given him right.

'Before, I'd have him not remove;
  Now, would not have him near;
With sacrifice I called on Love,
  And the apparition's Fear.'

Foolish to give it!—' 'Twas my whim,
  When he might parted be,
To think that I should stay by him
  In a little piece of me.

'He always said my hair was soft—
  What touches he will steal!
Each touch and look (and he'll look oft)
  I almost thought I'd feel.

'And then, when first he saw the hair,
    To think his dear amazement!
As if he wished from skies a star,
    And found it in his casement.

'He'd kiss the lock—and I had toyed
    With dreamed delight of this:
But ah, in proof, delight was void—
    I could not *see* his kiss!'

So, fond one, half this agony
    Were spared, which my hand hushes,
Could you have played, Sweet, the sweet spy,
    And blushed not for your blushes!

A GIRL'S SIN

II.—IN HIS EYES

Can I forget her cruelty
Who, brown miracle, gave you me?
Or with unmoisted eyes think on
The proud surrender overgone
(Lowlihead in haughty dress)
Of the tender tyranness?
And ere thou for my joy wast given,
How rough the road to that blest heaven!
With what pangs I fore-expiated
Thy cold outlawry from her head;
How was I trampled and brought low,
Because her virgin neck was so;

How thralled beneath the jealous state
She stood at point to abdicate;
How sacrificed, before to me
She sacrificed her pride and thee;
How did she, struggling to abase
Herself to do me strange, sweet grace,
Enforce unwitting me to share
Her throes and abjectness with her;
Thence heightening that hour when her lover
Her grace, with trembling, should discover,
And in adoring trouble be
Humbled at her humility!
And with what pitilessness was I
Afterslain, to pacify
The uneasy *manes* of her shame,
Her haunting blushes!—Mine the blame:
What fair injustice did I rue
For what I—did not tempt her to!
Nor aught the judging maid might win
Me to assoil from *her* sweet sin.
But naught were extreme punishment
For that beyond-divine content,
When my with-thee-first-giddied eyes
Stooped ere their due on Paradise!
O hour of consternating bliss
When I heavened me in thy kiss;
Thy softness (daring overmuch!)
Profanèd with my licensed touch;
Worshipped, with tears, on happy knee,
Her doubt, her trust, her shyness free,
Her timorous audacity!

LOVE DECLARED

I LOOKED, she drooped, and neither spake, and col̄
We stood, how unlike all forecasted thought
Of that desirèd minute! Then I leaned
Doubting; whereat she lifted—oh, brave eyes
Unfrighted:—forward like a wind-blown flame
Came bosom and mouth to mine!

                             That falling kiss
Touching long-laid expectance, all went up
Suddenly into passion; yea, the night
Caught, blazed, and wrapt us round in vibrant fire.

    Time's beating wing subsided, and the winds
Caught up their breathing, and the world's great pulse
Stayed in mid-throb, and the wild train of life
Reeled by, and left us stranded on a hush.
This moment is a statue unto Love
Carved from a fair white silence.

                            Lo, he stands
Within us—are we not one now, one, one roof,
His roof, and the partition of weak flesh
Gone down before him, and no more for ever?—
Stands like a bird new-lit, and as he lit,
Poised in our quiet being; only, only
Within our shaken hearts the air of passion,
Cleft by his sudden coming, eddies still
And whirs round his enchanted movelessness.
A film of trance between two stirrings! Lo,
It bursts; yet dream's snapped links cling round the limbs
Of waking: like a running evening stream
Which no man hears, or sees, or knows to run,

(Glazed with dim quiet,) save that there the moon
Is shattered to a creamy flicker of flame,
Our eyes' sweet trouble were hid, save that the love
Trembles a little on their impassioned calms.

THE WAY OF A MAID

THE lover whose soul shaken is
In some decuman billow of bliss,
Who feels his gradual-wading feet
Sink in some sudden hollow of sweet,
And 'mid love's usèd converse comes
Sharp on a mood which all joy sums,
An instant's fine compendium of
The liberal-leavèd writ of love—
His abashed pulses beating thick
At the exigent joy and quick,
Is dumbed, by aiming utterance great
Up to the miracle of his fate.

The wise girl, such Icarian fall
Saved by her confidence that she's small,—
As what no kindred word will fit
Is uttered best by opposite,
Love in the tongue of hate exprest,
And deepest anguish in a jest,—
Feeling the infinite must be
Best said by triviality,
Speaks, where expression bates its wings,
Just happy, alien, little things;
What of all words is in excess
Implies in a sweet nothingness;

With dailiest babble shows her sense
That full speech were full impotence;
And, while she feels the heavens lie **bare,**
She only talks about her hair.

BEGINNING OF END

She was aweary of the hovering
Of Love's incessant and tumultuous wing;
Her lover's tokens she would answer not—
'Twere well she should be strange with him **somewhat:**
A pretty babe, this Love,—but fie on it,
That would not suffer her lay it down a whit!
Appointed tryst defiantly she balked,
And with her lightest comrade lightly walked,
Who scared the chidden Love to hide apart,
And peep from some unnoticed corner of her **heart.**
She thought not of her lover, deem it not
(There yonder, in the hollow, that's *his* cot),
But she forgot not that he was forgot.
She saw him at his gate, yet stilled her tongue—
So weak she felt her, that she would feel strong,
And she must punish him for doing him **wrong:**
Passed, unoblivious of oblivion still;
And, if she turned upon the brow o' the hill,
It was so openly, so lightly done,
You saw she thought he was not thought upon.
He through the gate went back in bitterness;
She that night woke and stirred, with no distress,
Glad of her doing,—sedulous to be glad,
Lest perhaps her foolish heart suspect that it was **sad.**

PENELOPE

Love, like a wind, shook wide your blossomy eyes;
You trembled, and your breath came sobbing-wise,
  For that you loved me.

You were so kind, so sweet, none could withhold
To adore, but that you were so strange, so cold,
  For that you loved me.

Like to a box of spikenard did you break
Your heart about my feet. What words you spake!
  For that you loved me.

Life fell to dust without me; so you tried
All carefullest ways to drive me from your side,
  For that you loved me.

You gave yourself as children give, that weep
And snatch back, with—'I meant you not to keep!'
  For that you loved me.

I am no woman, girl, nor ever knew
That love could teach all ways that hate could do
  To her that loved me.

Have less of love, or less of woman in
Your love, or loss may even from this begin—
  That you so love me.

For, wild Penelope, the web you wove
You still unweave, unloving all your love.
  Is this to love me,

Or what rights have I that scorn could deny?
Even of your love, alas, poor Love must die,
    If so you love me!

THE END OF IT

SHE did not love to love, but hated him
For making her to love; and so her whim
From passion taught misprision to begin.
And all this sin
Was because love to cast out had no skill
Self, which was regent still.
Her own self-will made void her own self's will.

EPILOGUE

IF I have studied here in part
A tale as old as maiden's heart,
    'Tis that I do see herein
    Shadow of more piteous sin.

She, that but giving part, not whole,
Took even the part back, is the Soul:
    And that so disdainèd Lover—
    Best unthought, since Love is over.

To give the pledge, and yet be pined
That a pledge should have force to bind,
    This, O Soul, too often still
    Is the recreance of thy will!

Out of Love's arms to make fond chain,
And, because struggle bringeth pain,
        Hate Love for Love's sweet constraint,
        Is the way of Souls that faint.

Such a Soul, for saddest end,
Finds Love the foe in Love the friend;
        And—ah, grief incredible!—
        Treads the way of Heaven, to Hell.

ULTIMA

LOVE'S ALMSMAN PLAINETH HIS FARE

You, Love's mendicancy who never tried,
  How little of your almsman me you know!
Your little languid hand in mine you slide,
  Like to a child says—'Kiss me and let me go!'
And night for this is fretted with my tears,
  While I:—'How soon this heavenly neck doth tire,
Bending to me from its transtellar spheres!'
  Ah, heart all kneaded out of honey and fire!
Who bound thee to a body nothing worth,
  And shamed thee much with an unlovely soul,
That the most strainedest charity of earth
  Distasteth soon to render back the whole
Of thine inflamèd sweets and gentilesse?
  Whereat, like an unpastured Titan, thou
Gnaw'st on thyself for famine's bitterness,
  And leap'st against thy chain. Sweet Lady, how
Little a linking of the hand to you!
  Though I should touch yours careless for a year,
Not one blue vein would lie divinelier blue
  Upon your fragile temple, to unsphere
The seraphim for kisses! Not one curve
  Of your sad mouth would droop more sad and sweet.
But little food Love's beggars needs must serve,

That eye your plenteous graces from the street.
A hand-clasp I must feed on for a night,
  A noon, although the untasted feast you lay,
To mock me, of your beauty. That you might
  Be lover for one space, and make essay
What 'tis to pass unsuppered to your couch,
  Keep fast from love all day; and so be taught
The famine which these craving lines avouch!
  Ah! miser of good things that cost thee naught,
How know'st thou poor men's hunger?—Misery,
When I go doleless and unfed by thee!

A HOLOCAUST

*'No man ever attained supreme knowledge, unless his heart had
been torn up by the roots.'*

WHEN I presage the time shall come—yea, now
  Perchance is come, when you shall fail from me,
Because the mighty spirit, to whom you vow
  Faith of kin genius unrebukably,
Scourges my cloth; and from your side dismissed
  Henceforth this sad and most, most lonely soul
Must, marching fatally through pain and mist,
  The God-bid levy of its powers enrol;
When I presage that none shall hear the voice
  From the great Mount that clangs my ordained advance,
That sullen envy bade the churlish choice
  Yourself shall say, and turn your altered glance:—
O God! Thou knowest if this heart of flesh
  Quivers like broken entrails, when the wheel

Rolleth some dog in middle street, or fresh
   Fruit when ye tear it bleeding from the peel;
If my soul cries the uncomprehended cry
   When the red agony oozed on Olivet.
Yet not for this, a caitiff, falter I,
   Beloved whom I must lose, nor thence regret
The doubly-vouched and twin allegiance owed
   To you in Heaven, and Heaven in you, Lady.
How could you hope, loose dealer with my God,
   That I should keep for you my fealty?
For still 'tis thus:—because I am so true,
My Fair, to Heaven, I am so true to you!

MY LADY THE TYRANNESS

    Me since your fair ambition bows
    Feodary to those gracious brows,
    Is nothing mine will not confess
    Your sovran sweet rapaciousness?
    Though use to the white yoke inures,
    Half-petulant is
    Your loving rebel for somewhat his,
    Not yours, my love, not yours!

    Behold my skies, which make with me
    One passionate tranquillity!
    Wrap thyself in them as a robe,
    She shares them not; their azures probe,
    No countering wings thy flight endures.
    Nay, they do stole
    Me like an aura of her soul.
    I yield them, love, for yours!

But mine these hills and fields, which put
Not on the sanctity of her foot.
Far off, my dear, far off the sweet
Grave *pianissimo* of your feet!
My earth, perchance, your sway abjures?—
Your absence broods
O'er all, a subtler presence. Woods,
Fields, hills, all yours, all yours!

Nay then, I said, I have my thought,
Which never woman's reaching raught;
Being strong beyond a woman's might,
And high beyond a woman's height,
Shaped to my shape in all contours.—
I looked, and knew
No thought but you were garden to.
All yours, my love, all yours!

Meseemeth still, I have my life;
All-clement Her its resolute strife
Evades; contained, relinquishing
Her mitigating eyes; a thing
Which the whole girth of God secures.
Ah, fool, pause! pause!
I had no life, until it was
All yours, my love, all yours!

Yet, stern possession! I have my death,
Sole yielding up of my sole breath,
Which all within myself I die,
All in myself must cry the cry

Which the deaf body's wall immures.—
Thought fashioneth
My death without her.—Ah, even death
All yours, my love, all yours!

Death, then, be hers. I have my heaven,
For which no arm of hers has striven;
Which solitary I must choose,
And solitary win or lose.—
Ah, but not heaven my own endures!
I must perforce
Taste you, my stream, in God your source,—
So steep my heaven in yours!

At last I said—I have my God,
Who doth desire me, though a clod,
And from His liberal Heaven shall He
Bar in mine arms His privacy.
Himself for mine Himself assures.—
None shall deny
God to be mine, but He and I
All yours, my love, all yours!

I have no fear at all lest I
Without her draw felicity.
God for His Heaven will not forego
Her whom I found such heaven below,
And she will train Him to her lures.
Naught, lady, I love
In you but more is loved above;
What made me, makes Him, yours.

'I, thy sought own, am I forgot?'
Ha, thou?—thou liest, I seek thee not.
Why what, thou painted parrot, Fame,
What have I taught thee but her name?
Hear, thou slave Fame, while Time endures,
I give her thee;
Page her triumphal name!—Lady,
Take her, the thrall is yours.

UNTO THIS LAST

A BOY's young fancy taketh love
Most simply, with the rind thereof;
A boy's young fancy tasteth more
The rind, than the deific core.
Ah, Sweet! to cast away the slips
Of unessential rind, and lips
Fix on the immortal core, is well;
But heard'st thou ever any tell
Of such a fool would take for food
Aspect and scent, however good,
Of sweetest core Love's orchards grow?
Should such a phantast please him so,
Love where Love's reverent self denies
Love to feed, but with his eyes,
All the savour, all the touch,
Another's—was there ever such?
Such were fool, if fool there be;
Such fool was I, and was for thee!
But if the touch and savour too
Of this fruit—say, Sweet, of you—

You unto another give
For sacrosanct prerogative,
Yea, even scent and aspect were
Some elected Second's share;
And one, gone mad, should rest content
With memory of show and scent;
Would not thyself vow, if there sigh
Such a fool—say, Sweet, as I—
Treble frenzy it must be
Still to love, and to love thee?
Yet had I torn (man knoweth not,
Nor scarce the unweeping angels wot
Of such dread task the lightest part)
Her fingers from about my heart.
Heart, did we not think that she
Had surceased her tyranny?
Heart, we bounded, and were free!
O sacrilegious freedom!—Till
She came, and taught my apostate will
The winnowed sweet mirth cannot guess
And tear-fined peace of hopelessness;
Looked, spake, simply touched, and went.
Now old pain is fresh content,
Proved contents is unproved pain.
Pangs fore-tempted, which in vain
I, faithless, have denied, now bud
To untempted fragrance and the mood
Of contrite heavenliness; all days
Joy affrights me in my ways;
Extremities of old delight
Afflict me with new exquisite
Virgin piercings of surprise,—
Stung by those wild brown bees, her eyes!

ULTIMUM

Now in these last spent drops, slow, slower shed,
Love dies, Love dies, Love dies—ah, Love is dead!
Sad Love in life, sore Love in agony,
Pale Love in death; while all his offspring songs,
Like children, versed not in death's chilly wrongs,
About him flit, frightened to see him lie
So still, who did not know that Love could die.
One lifts his wing, where dulls the vermeil all
Like clotting blood, and shrinks to find it cold,
And when she sees its lapse and nerveless fall
Clasps her fans, while her sobs ooze through the webbèd
        gold.
Thereat all weep together, and their tears
Make lights like shivered moonlight on long waters.
Have peace, O piteous daughters!
He shall not wake more through the mortal years,
Nor comfort come to my soul widowèd,
Nor breath to your wild wings; for Love is dead!
I slew, that moan for him; he lifted me
Above myself, and that I might not be
Less than myself, need was that he should die;
Since Love that first did wing, now clogged me from the
        sky.
Yet lofty Love being dead thus passeth base—
There is a soul of nobleness which stays,
The spectre of the rose: be comforted,
Songs, for the dust that dims his sacred head!
The days draw on too dark for Song or Love;
O peace, my songs, nor stir ye any wing!
For lo, the thunder hushing all the grove,
And did Love live, not even Love could sing.

And, Lady, thus I dare to say,
Not all with you is passed away!
Beyond your star, still, still the stars are bright;
Beyond your highness, still I follow height;
Sole I go forth, yet still to my sad view,
Beyond your trueness, Lady, Truth stands true.
This wisdom sings my song with last firm breath,
Caught from the twisted lore of Love and Death,
The strange inwoven harmony that wakes
From Pallas' straying locks twined with her ægis-snakes:
'On him the unpetitioned heavens descend,
Who heaven on earth proposes not for end;
The perilous and celestial excess
Taking with peace, lacking with thankfulness.
Bliss in extreme befits thee not, until
Thou'rt not extreme in bliss; be equal still:
Sweets to be granted think thyself unmeet
Till thou have learned to hold sweet not too sweet.'
This thing not far is he from wise in art
Who teacheth; nor who doth, from wise in heart.

AN ANTHEM OF EARTH

PROEMION

IMMEASURABLE Earth!
Through the loud vast and populacy of Heaven,
Tempested with gold schools of ponderous orbs,
That cleav'st with deep-revolving harmonies
Passage perpetual, and behind thee draw'st
A furrow sweet, a cometary wake
Of trailing music! What large effluence,
Not sole the cloudy sighing of thy seas,
Nor thy blue-coifing air, encases thee
From prying of the stars, and the broad shafts
Of thrusting sunlight tempers? For, dropped near
From my removèd tour in the serene
Of utmost contemplation, I scent lives.
This is the efflux of thy rocks and fields,
And wind-cuffed forestage, and the souls of men,
And aura of all treaders over thee;
A sentient exhalation, wherein close
The odorous lives of many-throated flowers,
And each thing's mettle effused; that so thou wear'st,
Even like a breather on a frosty morn,
Thy proper suspiration. For I know,
Albeit, with custom-dulled perceivingness,
Nestled against thy breast, my sense not take

The breathings of thy nostrils, there's no tree,
No grain of dust, nor no cold-seeming stone,
But wears a fume of its circumfluous self.
Thine own life and the lives of all that live,
The issue of thy loins,
Is this thy gaberdine,
Wherein thou walkest through thy large demesne
And sphery pleasances,—
Amazing the unstalèd eyes of Heaven,
And us that still a precious seeing have
Behind this dim and mortal jelly.
                              Ah!
If not in all too late and frozen a day
I come in rearward of the throats of song,
Unto the deaf sense of the agèd year
Singing with doom upon me; yet give heed!
One poet with sick pinion, that still feels
Breath through the Orient gateways closing fast,
Fast closing t'ward the undelighted night!

ANTHEM

In nescientness, in nescientness,
Mother, we put these fleshly lendings on
Thou yield'st to thy poor children; took thy gift
Of life, which must, in all the after days,
Be craved again with tears,—
With fresh and still-petitionary tears.
Being once bound thine almsmen for that gift,
We are bound to beggary, nor our own can call
The journal dole of customary life,

But after suit obsequious for't to thee.
Indeed this flesh, O Mother,
A beggar's gown, a client's badging,
We find, which from thy hands we simply took,
Naught dreaming of the after penury,
In nescientness.
In a little joy, in a little joy,
We wear awhile thy sore insignia,
Nor know thy heel o' the neck. O Mother! Mother!
Then what use knew I of thy solemn robes,
But as a child to play with them? I bade thee
Leave thy great husbandries, thy grave designs,
Thy tedious state which irked my ignorant years,
Thy winter-watches, suckling of the grain,
Severe premeditation taciturn
Upon the brooded Summer, thy chill cares,
And all thy ministries majestical,
To sport with me, thy darling. Thought I not
Thou sett'st thy seasons forth processional
To pamper me with pageant,—thou thyself
My fellow-gamester, appanage of mine arms?
Then what wild Dionysia I, young Bacchanal,
Danced in thy lap! Ah for thy gravity!
Then, O Earth, thou rang'st beneath me,
Rocked to Eastward, rocked to Westward,
Even with the shifted
Poise and footing of my thought!
I brake through thy doors of sunset,
Ran before the hooves of sunrise,
Shook thy matron tresses down in fancies
Wild and wilful
As a poet's hand could twine them;

Caught in my fantasy's crystal chalice
The Bow, as its cataract of colours
Plashed to thee downward;
Then when thy circuit swung to nightward,
Night the abhorrèd, night was a new dawning,
Celestial dawning
Over the ultimate marges of the soul;
Dusk grew turbulent with fire before me,
And like a windy arras waved with dreams.
Sleep I took not for my bedfellow,
Who could waken
To a revel, an inexhaustible
Wassail of orgiac imageries;
Then while I wore thy sore insignia
In a little joy, O Earth, in a little joy;
Loving thy beauty in all creatures born of thee,
Children, and the sweet-essenced body of woman;
Feeling not yet upon my neck thy foot,
But breathing warm of thee as infants breathe
New from their mother's morning bosom. So I,
Risen from thee, restless winnower of the heaven,
Most Hermes-like, did keep
My vital and resilient path, and felt
The play of wings about my fledgèd heel—
Sure on the verges of precipitous dream,
Swift in its springing
From jut to jut of inaccessible fancies,
In a little joy.

In a little thought, in a little thought,
We stand and eye thee in a grave dismay,
With sad and doubtful questioning, when first

Thou speak'st to us as men: like sons who hear
Newly their mother's history, unthought
Before, and say—'She is not as we dreamed:
Ah me! we are beguiled!' What art thou, then,
That art not our conceiving? Art thou not
Too old for thy young children? Or perchance,
Keep'st thou a youth perpetual-burnishable
Beyond thy sons decrepit? It is long
Since Time was first a fledgeling;
Yet thou may'st be but as a pendant bulla
Against his stripling bosom swung. Alack!
For that we seem indeed
To have slipped the world's great leaping-time, and come
Upon thy pinched and dozing days: these weeds,
These corporal leavings, thou not cast'st us new,
Fresh from thy craftship, like the lilies' coats,
But foist'st us off
With hasty tarnished piecings negligent,
Snippets and waste
From old ancestral wearings,
That have seen sorrier usage; remainder-flesh
After our father's surfeits; nay with chinks,
Some of us, that, if speech may have free leave,
Our souls go out at elbows. We are sad
With more than our sires' heaviness, and with
More than their weakness weak; we shall not be
Mighty with all their mightiness, nor shall not
Rejoice with all their joy. Ay, Mother! Mother!
What is this Man, thy darling kissed and cuffed,
Thou lustingly engender'st,
To sweat, and make his brag, and rot,
Crowned with all honour and all shamefulness?

From nightly towers
He dogs the secret footsteps of the heavens,
Sifts in his hands the stars, weighs them as gold-dust,
And yet is he successive unto nothing
But patrimony of a little mold,
And entail of four planks. Thou hast made his mouth
Avid of all dominion and all mightiness,
All sorrow, all delight, all topless grandeurs,
All beauty, and all starry majesties,
And dim transtellar things;—even that it may,
Filled in the ending with a puff of dust,
Confess—'It is enough.' The world left empty
What that poor mouthful crams. His heart builded
For pride, for potency, infinity,
All heights, all deeps, and all immensities,
Arrased with purple like the house of kings,—
To stall the grey-rat, and the carrion-worm
Statelily lodge. Mother of mysteries!
Sayer of dark sayings in a thousand tongues,
Who bringest forth no saying yet so dark
As we ourselves, thy darkest! We the young,
In a little thought, in a little thought,
At last confront thee, and ourselves in thee,
And wake disgarmented of glory: as one
On a mount standing, and against him stands,
On the mount adverse, crowned with westering rays,
The golden sun, and they two brotherly
Gaze each on each;
He faring down
To the dull vale, his Godhead peels from him
Till he can scarcely spurn the pebble—
For nothingness of new-found mortality—

That mutinies against his gallèd foot.
Littly he sets him to the daily way,
With all around the valleys growing grave,
And known things changed and strange; but he holds on
Though all the land of light be widowèd,
In a little thought.

In a little strength, in a little strength,
We affront thy unveiled face intolerable,
Which yet we do sustain.
Though I the Orient never more shall feel
Break like a clash of cymbals, and my heart
Clang through my shaken body like a gong;
Nor ever more with spurted feet shall tread
I' the winepresses of song; naught's truly lost
That moulds to sprout forth gain: now I have on me
The high Phœbean priesthood, and that craves
An unrash utterance; not with flaunted hem
May the Muse enter in behind the veil,
Nor, though we hold the sacred dances good,
Shall the holy Virgins mænadize: ruled lips
Befit a votaress Muse.
Thence with no mutable, nor no gelid love,
I keep, O Earth, thy worship,
Though life slow, and the sobering Genius change
To a lamp his gusty torch. What though no more
Athwart its roseal glow
Thy face look forth triumphal? Thou putt'st on
Strange sanctities of pathos; like this knoll
Made derelict of day,
Couchant and shadowèd
Under dim Vesper's overloosened hair:

This, where embossèd with the half-blown seed
The solemn purple thistle stands in grass
Grey as an exhalation, when the bank
Holds mist for water in the nights of Fall.
Not to the boy, although his eyes be pure
As the prime snowdrop is
Ere the rash Phœbus break her cloister
Of sanctimonious snow;
Or Winter fasting sole on Himalay
Since those dove-nuncioed days
When Asia rose from bathing;
Not to such eyes,
Uneuphrasied with tears, the hierarchical
Vision lies unoccult, rank under rank
Through all create down-wheeling, from the Throne
Even to the bases of the pregnant ooze.
This is the enchantment, this the exaltation,
The all-compensating wonder,
Giving to common things wild kindred
With the gold-tesserate floors of Jove;
Linking such heights and such humilities
Hand in hand in ordinal dances,
That I do think my tread,
Stirring the blossoms in the meadow-grass,
Flickers the unwithering stars.
This to the shunless fardel of the world
Nerves my uncurbèd back: that I endure,
The monstrous Temple's moveless caryatid,
With wide eyes calm upon the whole of things,
In a little strength.

In a little sight, in a little sight,
We learn from what in thee is credible
The incredible, with bloody clutch and feet
Clinging the painful juts of jaggèd faith.
Science, old noser in its prideful straw,
That with anatomising scalpel tents
Its three-inch of thy skin, and brags 'All's bare'—
The eyeless worm, that, boring, works the soil,
Making it capable for the crops of God;
Against its own dull will
Ministers poppies to our troublous thought,
A Balaam come to prophecy,—parables,
Nor of its parable itself is ware,
Grossly unwotting; all things has expounded,
Reflux and influx, counts the sepulchre
The seminary of being, and extinction
The Ceres of existence: it discovers
Life in putridity, vigour in decay;
Dissolution even, and disintegration,
Which in our dull thoughts symbolize disorder,
Finds in God's thoughts irrefragable order,
And admirable the manner of our corruption
As of our health. It grafts upon the cypress
The tree of Life—Death dies on his own dart
Promising to our ashes perpetuity,
And to our perishable elements
Their proper imperishability; extracting
Medicaments from out mortality
Against too mortal cogitation; till
Even of the *caput mortuum* we do thus
Make a *memento vivere*. To such uses
I put the blinding knowledge of the fool,

Who in no order seeth ordinance;
Nor thrust my arm in nature shoulder-high,
And cry—'There's naught beyond!' How should I so,
That cannot with these arms of mine engirdle
All which I am; that am a foreigner
In mine own region? Who the chart shall draw
Of the strange courts and vaulty labyrinths,
The spacious tenements and wide pleasances,
Innumerable corridors far-withdrawn,
Wherein I wander darkling, of myself?
Darkling I wander, nor I dare explore
The long arcane of those dim catacombs,
Where the rat memory does its burrows make,
Close-seal them as I may, and my stolen tread
Starts populace, a *gens lucifuga;*
That too strait seems my mind my mind to hold,
And I myself incontinent of me.
Then go I, my foul-venting ignorance
With scabby sapience plastered, aye forsooth!
Clap my wise foot-rule to the walls o' the world,
And vow—*A goodly house, but something ancient,*
And I can find no Master? Rather, nay,
By baffled seeing, something I divine
Which baffles, and a seeing set beyond;
And so with strenuous gazes sounding down,
Like to the day-long porer on a stream,
Whose last look is his deepest, I beside
This slow perpetual Time stand patiently,
In a little sight.

In a little dust, in a little dust,
Earth, thou reclaim'st us, who do all our lives
Find of thee but Egyptian villeinage.
Thou dost this body, this enhavocked realm,
Subject to ancient and ancestral shadows;
Descended passions sway it; it is distraught
With ghostly usurpation, dinned and fretted
With the still-tyrannous dead; a haunted tenement,
Peopled from barrows and outworn ossuaries.
Thou giv'st us life not half so willingly
As thou undost thy giving; thou that teem'st
The stealthy terror of the sinuous pard,
The lion maned with curlèd puissance,
The serpent, and all fair strong beasts of ravin,
Thyself most fair and potent beast of ravin,
And thy great eaters thou, the greatest, eat'st.
Thou hast devoured mammoth and mastodon,
And many a floating bank of fangs,
The scaly scourges of thy primal brine,
And the tower-crested plesiosaure.
Thou fill'st thy mouth with nations, gorgest slow
On purple æons of kings; man's hulking towers
Are carcase for thee, and to modern sun
Disglutt'st their splintered bones.
Rabble of Pharaohs and Arsacidæ
Keep their cold house within thee; thou hast sucked down
How many Ninevehs and Hecatompyloi,
And perished cities whose great phantasmata
O'erbrow the silent citizens of Dis:—
Hast not thy fill?

Tarry awhile, lean Earth, for thou shalt drink,
Even till thy dull throat sicken,
The draught thou grow'st most fat on; hear'st thou not
The world's knives bickering in their sheaths? O patience!
Much offal of a foul world comes thy way,
And man's superfluous cloud shall soon be laid
In a little blood.

In a little peace, in a little peace,
Thou dost rebate thy rigid purposes
Of imposed being, and relenting, mend'st
Too much, with naught. The westering Phœbus' horse
Paws i' the lucent dust as when he shocked
The East with rising; O how may I trace
In this decline that morning when we did
Sport 'twixt the claws of newly-whelped existence,
Which had not yet learned rending? We did then
Divinely stand, not knowing yet against us
Sentence had passed of life, nor commutation
Petitioning into death. What's he that of
The Free State argues? Tellus, bid him stoop,
Even where the low *hic jacet* answers him;
Thus low, O Man! there's freedom's seignory,
Tellus' most reverend sole free commonweal,
And model deeply-policied: there none
Stands on precedence, nor ambitiously
Woos the impartial worm, whose favour kiss
With liberal largesse all; there each is free
To be e'en what he must, which here did strive
So much to be he could not; there all do
Their uses just, with no flown questioning.
To be took by the hand of equal earth

They doff her livery, slip to the worm,
Which lacqueys them, their suits of maintenance,
And, that soiled workaday apparel cast,
Put on condition: Death's ungentle buffet
Alone makes ceremonial manumission;
So are the heavenly statutes set, and those
Uranian tables of the primal Law.
In a little peace, in a little peace,
Like fierce beasts that a common thirst makes brothers,
We draw together to one hid dark lake;
In a little peace, in a little peace,
We drain with all our burthens of dishonour
Into the cleansing sands o' the thirsty grave.
The fiery pomps, brave exhalations,
And all the glistering shows o' the seeming world,
Which the sight aches at, we unwinking see
Through the smoked glass of Death; Death, wherewith's
        fined
The muddy wine of life; that earth doth purge
Of her plethora of man; Death, that doth flush
The cumbered gutters of humanity;
Nothing, of nothing king, with front uncrowned,
Whose hand holds crownets; playmate swart o' the strong;
Tenebrous moon that flux and refluence draws
Of the high-tided man; skull-housèd asp
That stings the heel of kings; true Fount of Youth,
Where he that dips is deathless; being's drone-pipe;
Whose nostril turns to blight the shrivelled stars,
And thicks the lusty breathing of the sun;
Pontifical Death, that doth the crevasse bridge
To the steep and trifid God; one mortal birth
That broker is of immortality.

Under this dreadful brother uterine,
This kinsman feared, Tellus, behold me come,
Thy son stern-nursed; who mortal-motherlike,
To turn thy weanlings' mouth averse, embitter'st
Thine over-childed breast. Now, mortal-sonlike,
I thou hast suckled, Mother, I at last
Shall sustenant be to thee. Here I untrammel,
Here I pluck loose the body's cementing,
And break the tomb of life; here I shake off
The bur o' the world, man's congregation shun,
And to the antique order of the dead
I take the tongueless vows: my cell is set
Here in thy bosom; my trouble is ended
In a little peace.

MISCELLANEOUS ODES

LAUS AMARA DOLORIS

IMPLACABLE sweet dæmon, Poetry,
What have I lost for thee!
Whose lips too sensitively well
Have shaped thy shrivelling oracle.
So much as I have lost, O world, thou hast,
And for thy plenty I am waste;
Ah, count, O world, my cost,
Ah, count, O world, thy gain,
For thou hast nothing gained but I have lost!
And ah, my loss is such,
If thou have gained as much
Thou hast even harvest of Egyptian years,
And that great overflow which gives thee grain—
The bitter Nilus of my risen tears!

I witness call the austere goddess, Pain,
Whose mirrored image trembles where it lies
In my confronting eyes,
If I have learned her sad and solemn scroll:—
Have I neglected her high sacrifice,
Spared my heart's children to the sacred knife,
Or turned her customed footing from my soul?
Yea, thou pale Ashtaroth who rul'st my life,

275

Of all my offspring thou hast had the whole.
One after one they passed at thy desire
To sacrificial sword, or sacrificial fire;
All, all,—save one, the sole.
One have I hid apart,
The latest-born and sweetest of my heart,
From thy requiring eyes.

O hope, most futile of futilities!
Thine iron summons comes again,
O inevadible Pain!
Not faithless to my pact, I yield:—'tis here,
That solitary and fair,
That most sweet, last, and dear;
Swerv'st thou? behold, I swerve not:—strike, nor spare!
Not my will shudders, but my flesh,
In awful secrecy to hear
The wind of thy great treading sweep afresh
Athwart my face, and agitate my hair.
The ultimate unnerving dearness take,
The extreme rite of abnegation make,
And sum in one all renderings that were.

The agony is done,
Her footstep passes on;—
The unchilded chambers of my heart rest bare.
The love, but not the loved, remains;
As where a flower has pressed a leaf
The page yet keeps the trace and stains.
For thy delight, world, one more grief,
My world, one loss more for thy gains!

Yet, yet, ye few, to whom is given
This weak singing, I have learned
Ill the starry roll of heaven,
Were this all that I discerned
Or of Poetry or of Pain.
Song! turn on thy hinge again!

Thine alternate panel showed,
Give the Ode a Palinode!
Pain, not thou an Ashtaroth,
Glutted with a bloody rite,
But the icy bath that doth
String the slack sinews loosened with delight.
O great Key-bearer and Keeper
Of the treasuries of God!
Wisdom's gifts are buried deeper
Than the arm of man can go,
Save thou show
First the way, and turn the sod.
The poet's crown, with misty weakness tarnished,
In thy golden fire is burnished
To round with more illustrious gleam his forehead.
And when with sacrifice of costliest cost
On my heart's altar is the Eterne adorèd,
The fire from heaven consumes the holocaust.
Nay, to vicegerence o'er the wide-confined
And mutinous principate of mans' restless mind
With thine anointing oils the singer is designed:
To that most desolate station
Thine is his deep and dolorous consecration.
Oh, where thy chrism shall dry upon my brow,
By that authentic sign I know

The sway is parted from this tenuous hand:
And all the wonted dreams that rankèd stand,
The high majestic state,
And cloud-consorting towers of visionary land,
To some young usurpation needs must go;
And I am all unsceptred of command.
Disdiademed I wait
To speak with sieging Death, mine enemy, in the gate.

Preceptress in the wars of God!
His tyros draw the unmortal sword,
And their celestial virtue exercise,
Beneath thy rigorous eyes.
Thou severe bride, with the glad suit adored
Of many a lover whose love is unto blood;
Every jewel in their crown
Thy lapidary hand does own;
Nor that warm jacinth of the heart can put
Its lustres forth, till it be cut.
Thou settest thine abode
A portress in the gateways of all love,
And tak'st the toll of joys; no maid is wed,
But thou dost draw the curtains of her bed.
Yea, on the brow of mother and of wife
Descends thy confirmation from above,
A Pentecostal flame; love's holy bread,
Consecrated,
Not sacramental is, but through thy leaven.

Thou pacest either frontier where our life
Marches with God's; both birth and death are given
Into thy lordship; those debated lands
Are subject to thy hands:

The border-warden, thou, of Heaven—
Yea, that same awful angel with the glaive
Which in disparadising orbit swept
Lintel and pilaster and architrave
Of Eden-gates, and forth before it drave
The primal pair, then first whose startled eyes,
With pristine drops o' the no less startled skies
Their own commingling, wept;—
With strange affright
Sin knew the bitter first baptismal rite.

Save through thy ministry man is not fed;
Thou uninvoked presid'st, and unconfest,
The mistress of his feast:
From the earth we gain our bread, and—like the bread
Dropt and regatheréd
By a child crost and thwart,
Whom need makes eat, though sorely weep he for't—
It tastes of dust and tears.

Iron Ceres of an earth where, since the Curse,
Man has had power perverse
Beside God's good to set his evil seed!
Those shining acres of the musket-spears—
Where flame and wither with swift intercease
Flowers of red sleep that not the corn-field bears—
Do yield thee minatory harvest, when
Unto the fallow time of sensual ease
Implacably succeed
The bristling issues of the sensual deed;
And like to meteors from a rotting fen

The fiery pennons flit o'er the stagnation
Of the world's sluggish and putrescent life,
Misleading to engulfing desolation
And blind, retributive, unguessing strife,
The fatal footsteps of pursuing men.
Thy pall in purple sovereignty was dipt
Beneath the tree of Golgotha;
And from the Hand, wherein the reed was clipt,
Thy bare and antique sceptre thou dost draw.
That God-sprung Lover to thy front allows,
Fairest, the bloody honour of His brows,
The great reversion of that diadem
Which did His drenched locks hem.
For the predestined Man of Grief,
O regnant Pain, to thee
His subject sway elected to enfeoff;
And from thy sad conferring to endure
The sanguine state of His investiture;
Yea, at thy hand, most sombre suzerain,
That dreadful crown He held in fealty;
O Queen of Calvary,
Holy and terrible, anointed Pain!

A CAPTAIN OF SONG

(ON A PORTRAIT OF COVENTRY PATMORE
BY J. S. SARGENT, R.A.)

Look on him. This is he whose works ye know;
Ye have adored, thanked, loved him,—no, not him!
But that of him which proud portentous woe
To its own grim

Presentment was not potent to subdue,
Nor all the reek of Erebus to dim.
This, and not him, ye knew.
Look on him now.   Love, worship if ye can,
The very man.
Ye may not. He has trod the ways afar,
The fatal ways of parting and farewell,
Where all the paths of painèd greatness are;
Where round and always round
The abhorrèd words resound,
The words accursed of comfortable men,—
'For ever'; and infinite glooms intolerable
With spacious replication give again,
And hollow jar,
The words abhorred of comfortable men.
You the stern pities of the gods debar
To drink where he has drunk—
The moonless mere of sighs,
And pace the places infamous to tell,
Where God wipes not the tears from any eyes,
Where-through the ways of dreadful greatness are.

He knows the perilous rout
That all those ways about
Sink into doom, and sinking, still are sunk.
And if his sole and solemn term thereout
He has attained, to love ye shall not dare
One who has journeyed there;
Ye shall mark well
The mighty cruelties which arm and mar
That countenance of control,
With minatory warnings of a soul

That hath to its own selfhood been most fell,
And is not weak to spare:
And lo, that hair
Is blanchèd with the travel-heats of hell.

If any be
That shall with rites of reverent piety
Approach this strong
Sad soul of sovereign Song,
Nor fail and falter with the intimate throng;
If such there be,
These, these are only they
Have trod the self-same way;
The never-twice revolving portals heard
Behind them clang infernal, and that word
Abhorrèd sighed of kind mortality,
As he—
Ah, even as he!

AGAINST URANIA

Lo, I, Song's most true lover, plain me sore
That worse than other women she can deceive,
For she being goddess, I have given her more
Than mortal ladies from their loves receive;
And first of her embrace
She was not coy, and gracious were her ways,
That I forgot all virgins to adore;
Nor did I greatly grieve
To bear through arid days
The pretty foil of her divine delays;

And one by one to cast
Life, love, and health,
Content, and wealth,
Before her, thinking ever on her praise,
Until at last
Naught had I left she would be gracious for.
Now of her cozening I complain me sore,
Seeing her uses,
That still, more constantly she is pursued,
And straitlier wooed,
Her only-adorèd favour more refuses,
And leaves me to implore
Remembered boon in bitterness of blood.

From mortal woman thou may'st know full well,
O poet, that dost deem the fair and tall
Urania of her ways not mutable,
What things shall thee befall
When thou art toilèd in her sweet, wild spell.
Do they strow for thy feet
A little tender favour and deceit
Over the sudden mouth of hidden hell?—
As more intolerable
Her pit, as her first kiss is heavenlier-sweet.
Are they, the more thou sigh,
Still the more watchful-cruel to deny?—
Know this, that in her service thou shalt learn
How harder than the heart of woman is
The immortal cruelty
Of the high goddesses.
True is his witness who doth witness this,
Whose gaze too early fell—

Nor thence shall turn,
Nor in those fires shall cease to weep and burn—
Upon her ruinous eyes and ineludible.

TO THE ENGLISH MARTYRS

Rain, rain on Tyburn tree,
Red rain a-falling;
Dew, dew on Tyburn tree,
Red dew on Tyburn tree,
And the swart bird a-calling.
The shadow lies on England now
Of the deathly-fruited bough:
Cold and black with malison
Lies between the land and sun;
Putting out the sun, the bough
Shades England now!

The troubled heavens do wan with care,
And burthened with the earth's despair
Shiver a-cold; the starvèd heaven
Has want, with wanting man bereaven.
Blest fruit of the unblest bough,
Aid the land that smote you, now!
That feels the sentence and the curse
Ye died if so ye might reverse.
When God was stolen from out man's mouth,
Stolen was the bread; then hunger and drouth
Went to and fro; began the wail,
Struck out the poor-house and the jail.
Ere cut the dykes, let through that flood,
Ye writ the protest with your blood;

Against this night—wherein our breath
Withers, and the toiled heart perisheth,—
Entered the *caveat* of your death,

Christ, in the form of His true Bride,
Again hung pierced and crucified,
And groaned, 'I thirst!' Not still ye stood,—
Ye had your hearts, ye had your blood;
And pouring out the eager cup,—
'The wine is weak, yet, Lord Christ, sup!'
Ah, blest! who bathed the parchèd Vine
With richer than His Cana-wine,
And heard, your most sharp supper past:
'Ye kept the best wine to the last!'

Ah, happy who
That sequestered secret knew,
How sweeter than bee-haunted dells
The blosmy blood of martyrs smells!
Who did upon the scaffold's bed,
The ceremonial steel between you, wed
With God's grave proxy, high and reverend **Death;**
Or felt about your neck, sweetly,
(While the dull horde
Saw but the unrelenting cord)
The Bridegroom's arm, and that long kiss
That kissed away your breath, and claimed **you Hi**
You did, with thrift of holy gain,
Unvenoming the sting of pain,
Hive its sharp heather-honey. **Ye**
Had sentience of the mystery

To make Abaddon's hookèd wings
Buoy you up to starry things;
Pain of heart, and pain of sense,
Pain the scourge, ye taught to cleanse;
Pain the loss became possessing;
Pain the curse was pain the blessing.
Chains, rack, hunger, solitude—these,
Which did your soul from earth release,
Left it free to rush upon
And merge in its compulsive Sun.
Desolated, bruised, forsaken,
Nothing taking, all things taken,
Lacerated and tormented,
The stifled soul, in naught contented,
On all hands straitened, cribbed, denied,
Can but fetch breath o' the Godward side.
Oh to me, give but to me
That flower of felicity,
Which on your topmost spirit ware
The difficult and snowy air
Of high refusal! and the heat
Of central love which fed with sweet
And holy fire i' the frozen sod
Roots that had ta'en hold on God.

Unwithering youth in you renewed
Those rosy waters of your blood,—
The true *Fons Juventutis;* ye
Pass with conquest that Red Sea,
And stretch out your victorious hand
Over the Fair and Holy Land.

O, by the Church's pondering art
Late set and named upon the chart
Of her divine astronomy,
Though your influence from on high
Long ye shed unnoted! Bright
New cluster in our Northern night,
Cleanse from its pain and undelight
An impotent and tarnished hymn,
Whose marish exhalations dim
Splendours they would transfuse! And thou
Kindle the words which blot thee now,
Over whose sacred corse unhearsed
Europe veiled her face, and cursed
The regal mantle grained in gore
Of genius, freedom, faith, and More!

Ah, happy Fool of Christ, unawed
By familiar sanctities,
You served your Lord at holy ease!
Dear Jester in the Courts of God—
In whose spirit, enchanting yet,
Wisdom and love, together met,
Laughed on each other for content!
That an inward merriment,
An inviolate soul of pleasure,
To your motions taught a measure
All your days; which tyrant king,
Nor bonds, nor any bitter thing
Could embitter or perturb;
No daughter's tears, nor, more acerb,
A daughter's frail declension from
Thy serene example, come

Between thee and thy much content.
Nor could the last sharp argument
Turn thee from thy sweetest folly;
To the keen *accolade* and holy
Thou didst bend low a sprightly knee,
And jest Death out of gravity
As a too sad-visaged friend;
So, jocund, passing to the end
Of thy laughing martyrdom;
And now from travel art gone home
Where, since gain of thee was given,
Surely there is more mirth in heaven!

Thus, in Fisher and in thee,
Arose the purple dynasty,
The anointed Kings of Tyburn tree;
High in act and word each one:
He that spake—and to the sun
Pointed—'I shall shortly be
Above yon fellow.' He too, he
No less high of speech and brave,
Whose word was: 'Though I shall have
Sharp dinner, yet I trust in Christ
To have a most sweet supper.' Priced
Much by men that utterance was
Of the doomed Leonidas,—
Not more exalt than these, which note
Men who thought as Shakespeare wrote.

But more lofty eloquence
That is writ by poets' pens
Lives in your great deaths: O these

Have more fire than poesies!
And more ardent than all ode,
The pomps and raptures of your blood!

By that blood ye hold in fee
This earth of England; Kings are ye:
And ye have armies—Want, and Cold,
And heavy Judgements manifold
Hung in the unhappy air, and Sins
That the sick gorge to heave begins,
Agonies, and Martyrdoms,
Love,. Hope, Desire, and all that comes
From the unwatered soul of man
Gaping on God. These are the van
Of conquest, these obey you; these,
And all the strengths of weaknesses,
That brazen walls disbed. Your hand,
Princes, put forth to the command,
And levy upon the guilty land
Your saving wars; on it go down,
Black beneath God's and heaven's frown;
Your prevalent approaches make
With unsustainable Grace, and take
Captive the land that captived you;
To Christ enslave ye and subdue
Her so bragged freedom: for the crime
She wrought on you in antique time,
Parcel the land among you: reign,
Viceroys to your sweet Suzerain!
Till she shall know
This lesson in her overthrow:
Hardest servitude has he

That's jailed in arrogant liberty;
And freedom, spacious and unflawed,
Who is walled about with God.

ODE FOR THE DIAMOND JUBILEE
OF QUEEN VICTORIA, 1897

NIGHT; and the street a corpse beneath the moon,
Upon the threshold of the jubilant day
That was to follow soon;
Thickened with inundating dark
'Gainst which the drowning lamps kept struggle; pole
And plank cast rigid shadows; 'twas a stark
Thing waiting for its soul,
The bones of the preluded pomp. I saw
In the cloud-sullied moon a pale array,
A lengthened apparition, slowly draw;
And as it came,
Brake all the streets in phantom flame
Of flag and flower and hanging, shadowy show
Of the to-morrow's glories, as might suit
A pageant of the dead; and spectral bruit
I heard, where stood the dead to watch the dead,
The long Victorian line that passed with printless tread.

First went the holy poets, two on two,
And music, sown along the hardened ground,
Budded like frequence of glad daisies, where
Those sacred feet did fare;
Arcadian pipe, and psaltery, around,
And stringèd viol, sound

To make for them melodious due.
In the first twain of those great ranks of death
Went One, the impress recent on his hair
Where it was dinted by the Laureate wreath:
Who sang those goddesses with splendours bare
On Ida hill, before the Trojan boy;
And many a lovely lay,
Where Beauty did her beauties unarray
In conscious song. I saw young Love his plumes deploy,
And shake their shivering lustres, till the night
Was sprinkled and bedropt with starry play
Of versicoloured light,
To see that Poet pass who sang him well;
And I could hear his heart
Throb like the after-vibrance of a bell.

A Strength beside this Beauty, Browning went,
With shrewd looks and intent,
And meditating still some gnarlèd theme.
Then came, somewhat apart,
In a fastidious dream,
Arnold, with a half-discontented calm,
Binding up wounds, but pouring in no balm.
The fervid breathing of Elizabeth
Broke on Christina's gentle-taken breath.
Rossetti, whose heart stirred within his breast
Like lightning in a cloud, a Spirit without rest,
Came on disranked; Song's hand was in his hair,
Lest Art should have withdrawn him from the band,
Save for her strong command;
And in his eyes high Sadness made its lair.

Last came a Shadow tall, with drooping lid,
Which yet not hid
The steel-like flashing of his armèd glance;
Alone he did advance,
And all the throngs gave room
For one that looked with such a captain's mien.
A scornful smile lay keen
On lips that, living, prophesied of doom;
His one hand held a lightning-bolt, the other
A cup of milk and honey blent with fire;
It seemed as in that quire
He had not, nor desired not, any brother.
A space his alien eye surveyed the pride
Of meditated pomp, as one that much
Disdained the sight, methought; then, at a touch,
He turned the heel, and sought with shadowy stride
His station in the dim,
Where the sole-thoughted Dante waited him.

What throngs illustrious next, of Art and Prose,
Too long to tell! But other music rose
When came the sabre's children: they who led
The iron-throated harmonies of war,
The march resounding of the armèd line,
And measured movement of battalia:
Accompanied their tread
No harps, no pipes of soft Arcadia,
But—borne to me afar—
The tramp of squadrons, and the bursting mine,
The shock of steel, the volleying rifle-crack,
And echoes out of ancient battles dead.
So Cawnpore unto Alma thundered back,
And Delhi's cannon roared to Gujerat:

Carnage through all those iron vents gave out
Her thousand-mouthèd shout.
As balefire answering balefire is unfurled,
From mountain-peaks, to tell the foe's approaches,
So ran that battle-clangour round the world,
From famous field to field
So that reverberated war was tossed;
And—in the distance lost—
Across the plains of France and hills of Spain
It swelled once more to birth,
And broke on me again,
The voice of England's glories girdling in the earth.

It caught like fire the main,
Where rending planks were heard, and broadsides pealed,
That shook were all the seas,
Which feared, and thought on Nelson. For with them
That struck the Russ, that brake the Mutineer,
And smote the stiff Sikh to his knee,—with these
Came they that kept our England's sea-swept hem,
And held afar from her the foreign fear.
After them came
They who pushed back the ocean of the Unknown,
And fenced some strand of knowledge for our own
Against the outgoing sea
Of ebbing mystery;
And on their banner 'Science' blazoned shone.
The rear were they that wore the statesman's fame,
From Melbourne, to
The arcane face of the much-wrinkled Jew.

Lo, in this day we keep the yesterdays,
And those great dead of the Victorian line.
They passed, they passed, but cannot pass away,
For England feels them in her blood like wine.
She was their mother, and she is their daughter,
This Lady of the water,
And from their loins she draws the greatness which they
    were.
And still their wisdom sways,
Their power lives in her.
Their thews it is, England, that lift thy sword,
They are the splendour, England, in thy song,
They sit unbidden at thy council-board,
Their fame does compass all thy coasts from wrong,
And in thy sinews they are strong.
Their absence is a presence and a guest
In this day's feast;
This living feast is also of the dead,
And this, O England, is thine All Souls' Day.
And when thy cities flake the night with flames,
Thy proudest torches yet shall be their names.

O royal England! happy child
Of such a more than regal line;
Be it said
Fair right of jubilee is thine;
And surely thou art unbeguiled
If thou keep with mirth and play,
With dance, and jollity, and praise,
Such a To-day which sums such Yesterdays.
Pour to the joyless ones thy joy, thy oil
And wine to such as faint and toil.

And let thy vales make haste to be more green
Than any vales are seen
In less auspicious lands,
And let thy trees clap all their leafy hands,
And let thy flowers be gladder far of hue
Than flowers of other regions may;
Let the rose, with her fragrance sweetened through,
Flush as young maidens do,
With their own inward blissfulness at play.
And let the sky twinkle an eagerer blue
Over our English isle
Than any otherwhere;
Till strangers shall behold, and own that she is fair.
Play up, play up, ye birds of minstrel June,
Play up your reel, play up your giddiest spring,
And trouble every tree with lusty tune,
Whereto our hearts shall dance
For overmuch pleasance,
And children's running make the earth to sing.
And ye soft winds, and ye white-fingered beams,
Aid ye her to invest,
Our queenly England, in all circumstance
Of fair and feat adorning to be drest;
Kirtled in jocund green,
Which does befit a Queen,
And like our spirits cast forth lively gleams:
And let her robe be goodly garlanded
With store of florets white and florets red,
With store of florets white and florets gold,
A fair thing to behold;
Intrailed with the white blossom and the blue,
A seemly thing to view!

And thereunto,
Set over all a woof of lawny air,
From her head wavering to her sea-shod feet,
Which shall her lovely beauty well complete,
And grace her much to wear.

Lo, she is dressed, and lo, she cometh forth,
Our stately Lady of the North;
Lo, how she doth advance,
In her most sovereign eye regard of puissance,
And tiar'd with conquest her prevailing brow,
While nations to her bow.
Come hither, proud and ancient East,
Gather ye to this Lady of the North,
And sit down with her at her solemn feast,
Upon this culminant day of all her days;
For ye have heard the thunder of her goings-forth,
And wonder of her large imperial ways.
Let India send her turbans, and Japan
Her pictured vests from that remotest isle
Seated in the antechambers of the Sun:
And let her Western sisters for a while
Remit long envy and disunion,
And take in peace
Her hand behind the buckler of her seas,
'Gainst which their wrath has splintered; come, for she
Her hand ungauntlets in mild amity.

Victoria! Queen, whose name is victory,
Whose woman's nature sorteth best with peace,
Bid thou the cloud of war to cease

Which ever round thy wide-girt empery
Fumes, like to smoke about a burning brand,
Telling the energies which keep within
The light unquenched, as England's light shall be;
And let this day hear only peaceful din.
For, queenly woman, thou art more than woman;
Thy name the often-struck barbarian shuns:
Thou art the fear of England to her foemen,
The love of England to her sons.
And this thy glorious day is England's; who
Can separate the two?
She joys thy joys and weeps thy tears,
And she is one with all thy moods;
Thy story is the tale of England's years,
And big with all her ills, and all her stately goods.
Now unto thee
The plenitude of the glories thou didst sow
Is garnered up in prosperous memory;
And, for the perfect evening of thy day,
An untumultuous bliss, serenely gay,
Sweetened with silence of the after-glow.
Nor does the joyous shout
Which all our lips give out
Jar on that quietude; more than may do
A radiant childish crew,
With well-accordant discord fretting the soft hour,
Whose hair is yellowed by the sinking blaze
Over a low-mouthed sea. Exult, yet be not twirled,
England, by gusts of mere
Blind and insensate lightness; neither fear
The vastness of thy shadow on the world.

If in the East
Still strains against its leash the unglutted beast
Of War; if yet the cannon's lip be warm;
Thou, whom these portents warn but not alarm,
Feastest, but with thy hand upon the sword,
As fits a warrior race:
Not like the Saxon fools of olden days,
With the mead dripping from the hairy mouth,
While all the South
Filled with the shaven faces of the Norman horde.

THE NINETEENTH CENTURY

As, fore-announced by threat of flame and smoke,
Out of the night's lair broke
The sun among the startled stars, whose blood
Looses its slow bright flood
Beneath the radiant onset of the sun;
So crouches he anon,
With nostrils breathing threat of smoke and flame,
Back to the lairing night wherefrom he came.

Say, who is she,
With cloudy battle smoking round her feet,
That goes out through the exit-doors of death;
And at the alternate limit of her path,
Where first her nascent footsteps troubled day,
Forgotten turmoil curls itself away?
Who is she that rose
Tumultuous, and in tumult goes?

This is she
That rose 'midst dust of a down-tumbled world,
And dies with rumour on the air
Of preparation
For a more ample devastation,
And death of ancient fairness no more fair.
First when she knew the day,
The holy poets sung her on her way:
The high, clear band that takes
Its name from heaven-acquainted mountain-lakes;
And he
That like a star set in Italian sea;
And he that mangled by the jaws of our
Fierce London, from all frets
Lies balmed in Roman violets;
And other names of power,
Too recent but for worship and regret,
On whom the tears lie wet.

But not to these
She gave her heart; her heart she gave
To the blind worm that bores the mold,
Bloodless, pertinacious, cold,
Unweeting what itself upturns,
The seer and prophet of the grave.
It reared its head from off the earth
(Which gives it life and gave it birth)
And placed upon its eyeless head a crown,
Thereon a name writ new,
'Science,' erstwhile with ampler meanings known;
And all the peoples in their turns
Before the blind worm bowed them down.

Yet, crowned beyond its due,
Working dull way by obdurate, slow degrees,
It is a thing of sightless prophecies;
And glories, past its own conceit,
Wait to complete
Its travail, when the mounded time is meet.
Nor measured, fit renown,
When that hour paces forth,
Shall overlook those workers of the North
And West, those patient Darwins who forthdrew
From humble dust what truth they knew,
And greater than they knew, not knowing all they knew.
Yet was their knowledge in its scope a Might,
Strong and true souls to measure of their sight.
Behold the broad globe in their hands comprest,
As a boy kneads a pellet, till the East
Looks in the eyes o' the West;
And as guest whispers guest
That counters him at feast,
The Northern mouth
Leans to the attent ear of the blended South.
The fur-skinned garb justling the Northern Bear
Crosses the threshold where,
With linen wisp girt on,
Drowses the next-door neighbour of the sun.
Such their laborious worth
To change the old face of the wonted earth.

Nor were they all o' the dust; as witness may
Davy and Faraday;
And they
Who clomb the cars

And learned to rein the chariots of the stars;
Or who in night's dark waters dipt their hands
To sift the hid gold from its sands;
And theirs the greatest gift, who drew to light
By their sciential might,
The secret ladder, wherethrough all things climb
Upward from the primeval slime.

Nor less we praise
Him that with burnished tube betrays
The multitudinous diminutive
Recessed in virtual night
Below the surface-seas of sight;
Him whose enchanted windows give
Upon the populated ways
Where the shy universes live
Ambushed beyond the unapprehending gaze:
The dusted anther's globe of spiky stars;
The beetle flashing in his minute mail
Of green and golden scale;
And every water-drop a-sting with writhing wars.
The unnoted green scale cleaving to the moist earth's face
Behold disclosed a conjugal embrace,
And womb—
Submitting to the tomb—
That sprouts its lusty issue:* everywhere conjoins
Either glad sex, and from unguessed-at loins
Breeds in an opulent ease
The liberal earth's increase;

* The prothallus of the fern, for example, which contains in
itself the two sexes, and decays as the young fern sprouts
from it.

Such Valentine's sweet unsurmisèd diocese.
Nor, dying Lady, of the sons
Whom proudly owns
Thy valedictory and difficult breath,
The least are they who followed Death
Into his obscure fastnesses,
Tracked to her secret lair Disease—

Under the candid-seeming and confederate Day
Venoming the air's pure lips to kiss and to betray;
Who foiled the ancient Tyrant's grey design
Unfathomed long, and brake his dusty toils,
Spoiling him of his spoils,
And man, the loud dull fly, loosed from his woven line.
Such triumph theirs who at the destined term
Descried the arrow flying in the day—
The age-long hidden Germ—
And threw their prescient shield before its deadly way.

Thou, spacious Century!
Hast seen the Western knee
Set on the Asian neck,
The dusky Africa
Kneel to imperial Europe's beck;
The West for her permitted while didst see
Stand mistress-wise and tutelar
To the grey nations dreaming on their days afar,
From old forgotten war
Folding hands whence has slid disusèd rule;
The while, unprescient, in her regent school
She shapes the ample days and things to be,
And large new empery.

Thence Asia shall be brought to bed
Of dominations yet undreamed;
Narrow-eyed Egypt lift again the head
Whereon the far-seen crown Nilotic gleamed.
Thou'st seen the Saxon horde whose veins run brine,
Spawned of the salt wave, wet with the salt breeze,
    Their sails combine,
Lash their bold prows together, and turn swords
Against the world's knit hordes;
The whelps repeat the lioness' roar athwart the windy seas.

Yet let it grieve, grey Dame,
Thy passing spirit, God wot,
Thou wast half-hearted, wishing peace, but not
The means of it. The avaricious flame
Thou'st fanned, which thou should'st tame:
Cluckd'st thy wide brood beneath thy mothering plumes,
    And coo'dst them from their fumes,
Stretched necks provocative, and throats
Ruffled with challenging notes;
    Yet all didst mar,
Flattering the too-much-pampered Boy of War:
Whence the far-jetting engine, and the globe
In labour with her iron progeny,—
Infernal litter of sudden-whelpèd deaths,
    Vomiting venomous breaths;
The growl as of long surf that draweth back
Half a beach in its rattling track,
    When like a tiger-cat
    The angry rifle spat
Its fury in the opposing foeman's eyes;—
These are thy consummating victories,
For this hast thou been troubled to be wise!

And now what child is this upon thy lap,
Born in the red glow of relighted war?
That draws Bellona's pap,
—Fierce foster-mother!—does already stare
With mimicked dark regard
And copied threat of brow whose trick it took from her:
Young Century, born to hear
The cannon talking at its infant ear—
The Twentieth of Time's loins, since that
Which in the quiet snows of Bethlehem he begat.
Ah! with forthbringing such and so ill-starred,
After the day of blood and night of fate,
Shall it survive with brow no longer marred,
Lip no more wry with hate;
With all thou hadst of good,
But from its blood
Washed thine hereditary ill,
Yet thy child still?

PEACE

ON THE TREATY IN SOUTH AFRICA IN 1902

Peace:—as a dawn that flares
Within the brazier of the barrèd East,
Kindling the ruinous walls of storm surceased
To rent and roughened glares,
After such night when lateral wind and rain
Torment the to-and-fro perplexèd trees
With thwart encounter; which, of fixture strong,

Take only strength from the endurèd pain:
And throat by thoat begin
The birds to make adventure of sweet din,
Till all the forest prosper into song:—
    Peace, even such a peace,
(O be my words an auspice!) dawns again
Upon our England, from her lethargies
Healed by that baptism of *her* cleansing pain.

Ended, the long endeavour of the land:
Ended, the set of manhood towards the sand
Of thirsty death; and their more deadly death,
Who brought back only what they fain had lost,
No more worth-breathing breath,—
Gone the laborious and use-working hand.
Ended, the patient drip of women's tears,
Which joined the patient drip of faithful blood
To make of blood and water the sore flood
That pays our conquest's costliest cost.
This day, if fate dispose,
Shall make firm friends from firm and firm-met foes.
And now, Lord, since Thou hast upon hell's floor
Bound, like a snoring sea, the blood-drowsed bulk of War,
Shall we not cry, on recognising knees,
This is Thy peace?

If, England, it be but to lay
The heavy head down, the old heavy way;
Having a space awakened and been bold
To break from them that had thee in the snare,—
Resume the arms of thy false Dalila, Gold,
Shameful and nowise fair:

Forget thy sons who have lain down in bed
With Dingaan and old dynasties, nor heed
The ants that build their empires overhead;
Forget their large in thy contracted deed,
And that thou stand'st twice-pledged to being great
For whom so many children greatly bleed,
Trusting thy greatness with their deaths: if thou,
England, incapable of proffered fate,
See in such deaths as these
But purchased pledges of unhindered mart,
And hirelings spent that in thy ringed estate
For some space longer now
Thou mayst add gain to gain, and take thine ease,—
God hast made hard thy heart;
Thou hast but bought thee respite, nor surcease.
Lord, this is not Thy peace!

But wilt thou, England, stand
With vigilant heart and prescient brain?—
Knowing there is no peace
Such as fools deem, of equal-balanced ease:—
That they who build the State
Must, like the builders of Jerusalem,
The trowel in their hand,
Work with the sword laid ever nigh to them.
If thou hold Honour worthy gain
At price of gold and pain;
And all thy sail and cannon somewhat more
Than the fee'd watchers of the rich man's store.
If thou discern the thing which all these ward
Is that imperishable thing, a Name,

And that Name, England, which alone is lord
Where myriad-armèd India owns with awe
A few white faces; uttered forth in flame
Where circling round the earth
Has English battle roared;
Deep in mid-forest African a Law;
That in this Name's small girth
The treasure is, thy sword and navies guard:
If thou wilt crop the specious sins of ease,
Whence still is War's increase,—
Proud flesh which asks for War, the knife of God,
Save to thyself, thyself use cautery;
Wilt stay the war of all with all at odd
And teach thy jarring sons
Truth innate once,—
That in the whole alone the part is blest and great.
O should this fire of war thus purge away
The inveterate stains of too-long ease,
And yield us back our Empire's clay
Into one shoreless State
Compact and hardened for its uses: these
No futile sounds of joyance are to-day;—
Lord, unrebuked we may
Call this Thy peace!

And in this day be not
Wholly forgot
They that made possible but shall not see
Our solemn jubilee.
Peace most to them who lie
Beneath unnative sky;

In whose still hearts is dipt
Our reconciling script:
Peace! But when shouts shall start the housetop bird
let those that speak not, be the loudest heard!

CECIL RHODES

DIED MARCH 26, 1902

THEY that mis-said
This man yet living, praise him dead.
And I too praise, yet not the baser things
Wherewith the market and the tavern rings.
Not that high things for gold,
He held, were bought and sold,
That statecraft's means approved are by the end;
Not for all which commands
The loud world's clapping hands,
To which cheap press and cheaper patriots bend;
But for the dreams,
For those impossible gleams
He half made possible; for that he was
Visioner of vision in a most sordid day:
This draws
Back to me Song long alien and astray.

In dreams what did he not,
Wider than his wide deeds? In dreams he wrought
What the old world's long livers must in act forego.
From the Zambesi to the Limpopo
He the many-languaged land

Took with his large compacting hand
And pressed into a nation: 'thwart the accurst
And lion-'larumed ways,
Where the lean-fingered Thirst
Wrings at the throat, and Famine strips the bone;
A tawny land, with sun at sullen gaze,
And all above a cope of heated stone;
He heard the shirted miner's rough halloo
Call up the mosquèd Cairene; harkened clear
The Cairene's far-off summons sounding through
The sea's long noises to the Capeman's ear.

He saw the Teuton and the Saxon grip
Hands round the warded world, and bid it rock,
While they did watch its cradle. Like a ship
It swung, whileas the cabined inmates slept,
Secure their peace was kept,
Such arms of warranty about them lock.
Ophir* he saw, her long-ungazed-at gold,
Stirred from its deep

And often-centuried sleep,
Wink at the new Sun in an English hold;
England, from Afric's swarty loins
Drawing fecundity,
Wax to the South and North,
To East and West increase her puissant goings-forth,
And strike young emperies, like coins,
In her own recent effigy.
He saw the three-branched Teuton hold the sides

* Rhodesia, according to some modern views.

Of the round world, and part it as a dish
Whereof to each his wish
The amity of the full feast decides.

So large his dreams, so little come to act!
Who must call on the cannon to compact
The hard Dutch-stubborned land,
Seditious even to such a potent hand;
Who grasped and held his Ophir: held, no less,
The Northern ways, but never lived to see
The wing-foot messages
Dart from the Delta to the Southern Sea;
Who, confident of gold,
A leaner on the statesman's arts
And the unmartial conquests of the marts,
Died with the sound of battle round him rolled,
And rumour of battle in all nations' hearts;
Dying, saw his life a thing
Of large beginnings; and for young
Hands yet untrained the harvesting,
Amid the iniquitous years if harvest sprung.

So in his death he sowed himself anew;
Cast his intents over the grave to strike
In the left world of livers living roots,
And, banyan-like,
From his one tree raise up a wood of shoots.
The indestructible intents which drew
Their sap from him
Thus, with a purpose grim,
Into strange lands and hostile yet he threw,

That there might be
From him throughout the earth posterity:
And so did he—
Like to a smouldering fire by wind-blasts swirled—
His dying embers strew to kindle all the world.

Yet not for this I praise
The ending of his strenuous days;
No, not alone that still
Beyond the grave stretched that imperial Will:
But that Death seems
To set the gateway wide to ampler dreams.
Yea, yet he dreams upon Matoppo hill,
The while the German and the Saxon see,
And seeing, wonder,
The spacious dreams take shape and be,
As at compulsion of his sleep thereunder.
Lo, young America at the Mother's knee,
Unlearning centuried hate,
For love's more blest extreme;
And this is his dream,
And sure the dream is great.
Lo, Colonies on Colonies,
The furred Canadian and the digger's shirt,
To the one Mother's skirt
Cling, in the lore of Empire to be wise;
A hundred wheels a-turn
All to one end—that England's sons may learn
The glory of their sonship, the supreme
Worth that befits the heirs of such estate.
All these are in his dream,
And sure the dream is great.

So, to the last
A visionary vast,
The aspirant soul would have the body lie
Among the hills immovably exalt
As he above the crowd that haste and halt,
'Upon that hill which I
Called "View of All the World" '; to show thereby
That still his unappeasable desires
Beneath his feet surveyed the peoples and empires.
Dreams, haply of scant worth,
Bound by our little thumb-ring of an earth;
Yet an exalted thing
By the gross search for food and raimenting.
So in his own Matoppos, high, aloof,
The elements for roof,
Claiming his mountain kindred, and secure,
Within that sepulture
Stern like himself and unadorned,
From the loud multitude he ruled and scorned,
There let him cease from breath,—
Alone in crowded life, not lonelier in death.

OF NATURE: LAUD AND PLAINT

Lo, here stand I and Nature, gaze to gaze,
And I the greater. Couch thou at my feet,
Barren of heart, and beautiful of ways,
Strong to weak purpose, fair and brute-brained beast.
I am not of thy fools
Who goddess thee with impious flatteries sweet,
Stolen from the little Schools

Which cheeped when that great mouth of Rydal ceased.
A little suffer that I try
What thou art, Child, and what am I—
Thy younger, forward brother, subtle and small,
As thou art gross and of thy person great withal.

Behold, the child
With Nature needs not to be reconciled.
The babe that keeps the womb
Questions not if with love
The life, distrainèd for its uses, come;
Nor we demand, then, of
The Nature who is in us and around us,
Whose life doth compass, feed, and bound us,
What prompteth her to bless
With gifts, unknown for gifts, our innocent thanklessness.
Mother unguessed is she, to whom
We still are in the womb.
Then comes the incidental day
When our young mouth is weaned; and from her arms we
        stray.
'Tis over; not, mistake me not,
Those divine gleams forgot
Which one with a so ampler mouth hath sung;
Not of these sings
My weak endeavouring tongue;
But of those simpler things
Less heavenful: the unstrained integrity
Moving most natively,
As the glad customed lot
Of birthright privilege allows,
Through the domestic chambers of its Father's house;

The virgin hills, provoking to be trod;
The cloud, the stream, the tree,
The allowing bosom of the warm-breathed sod—
No alien and untemptable delight.
The wonder in a wondrous sight
Was wondrous simple, as our simple God—
Yet not dulled, daily, base,
But sweet and safe possession as our mother's face,
Which we knew not for sweet, but sweetly had;
For who says—'Lo, how sweet!' has first said—'Lo, how
    sad!'

This, not to be regained with utmost sighs,
This unconsidered birthright, is made void
As Edom's, and destroyed.
Grown man, we now despise
Thee, known for woman, nor too wise;
As still the mother human
Is known for not too wise, and even woman.
We take ingrateful, for a blinded while,
Thine ignorant, sweet smile.
Yield maids their eyes unto their lovers' gaze?—
Why, so dost thou. And is their gracious favour
Doled but to draw us on through warpèd ways,
Delays behind delays,
To tempt with scent,
And to deny the savour?—
Ah, Lady, if that vengeanec were thy bent,
Woman should 'venge thee for thy scornèd smiles:
Her ways are as thy ways,
Her wiles are as thy wiles.

No second joy; one only first and over,
Which all life wanders from and looks back to;
For sweet too sweet, till sweet is past recover:—
Let bitter Love and every bitter lover
Say, *Love's not bitter*, if I speak not true.
The first kiss to repeat!
The first 'Mine only Sweet!'
Thine only sweet that sweetness, very surely,
And a sour truth thou spakest, if thou knew.
That first kiss to restore
By Nature given so frankly, taken so securely!
To knit again the broken chain; once more
To run and be to the Sun's bosom caught;
Over life's bended brows prevail
With laughters of the insolent nightingale,
Jocund of heart in darkness; to be taught
Once more the daisy's tale,
And hear each sun-smote buttercup clang bold,
A beaten gong of gold;
To call delaying Phœbus up with chanticleer;
Once more, once more to see the Dawn unfold
Her rosy bosom to the married Sun;
Fulfilled with his delight,
Perfected in sweet fear—
Sweet fear, that trembles for sweet joy begun
As slowly drops the swathing night,
And all her barèd beauty lies warm-kissed and won!

No extreme rites of penitence avail
To lighten thee of knowledge, to impart
Once more the language of the daisy's tale,
And that doctorial Art

Of knowing-not to thine oblivious heart!
Of all the vain
Words of man's mouth, there are no words so vain
As 'once more' and 'again'!
Hope not of Nature; she nor gives nor teaches;
She suffers thee to take
But what thine own hand reaches,
And can itself make sovereign for thine ache.
Ah, hope not her to heal
The ills she cannot feel,
Or dry with many-businessed hand the tear
Which never yet was weak
In her unfretted eyes, on her uncarkèd cheek.

O heart of Nature! did man ever hear
Thy yearned-for word, supposèd dear?—
His pleading voice returns to him alone;
He hears none other tone.
No, no;
Take back, O poets, your praises little-wise,
Nor fool weak hearts to their unshunned distress,
Who deem that even after your device
They shall lie down in Nature's holiness:
For it was never so;
She has no hands to bless.
Her pontiff thou; she looks to thee,
O man; she has no use, nor asks not, for thy knee,
Which but bewilders her,
Poor child; nor seeks thy fealty,
And those divinities thou wouldst confer.
If thou wouldst bend in prayer,
Arise, pass forth; thou must look otherwhere.

Thy travail all is null;
This Nature fair,
This gate is closèd, this Gate Beautiful,—
No man shall go in there,
Since the Lord God did pass through it;
'Tis sealed unto the King,
The King Himself shall sit
Therein, with them that are His following.
Go, leave thy labour null;
Ponder this thing.

Lady divine!
That giv'st to men good wine,
And yet the best thou hast
And nectarous, keepest to the last,
And bring'st not forth before the Master's sign:—
How few there be thereof that ever taste,
Quaffing in brutish haste,
Without distinction of thy great repast!
For ah, this Lady I have much miscalled;
Nor fault in her, but in thy wooing is;
And her allowèd lovers that are installed,
Find her right frank of her sweet heart, y-wis.
Then if thy wooing thou aright wouldst 'gin,
Lo here the door; strait and rough-shapen 'tis,
And scant they be that ever here make stays,
But do the lintel miss,
In dust of these blind days.
Knock, tarry thou, and knock,
Although it seem but rock:
Here is the door where thou must enter in
To heart of Nature and of Woman too,

And olden things made new.
Stand at the door and knock;
For it unlocked
Shall all locked things unlock,
And win but here, thou shalt to all things win,
And thou no more be mocked.
For know, this Lady Nature thou hast left,
Of whom thou fear'st thee reft,
This Lady is God's Daughter, and she lends
Her hand but to His friends,
But to her Father's friends the hand which thou wouldst
    win;
Then enter in,
And here is that which shall for all make mends.

SONNETS

AD AMICAM

I

Dear Dove, that bear'st to my sole-labouring ark
  The olive-branch of so long wishèd rest,
When the white solace glimmers through my dark
  Of nearing wings, what comfort in my breast!
Oh, may that doubted day not come, not come,
  When you shall fail, my heavenly messenger,
And drift into the distance and the doom
  Of all my impermissible things that were!
Rather than so, now make the sad farewell,
  Which yet may be with not too-painèd pain,
Lest I again the acquainted tale should tell
  Of sharpest loss that pays for shortest gain.
    Ah, if my heart should hear no white wings thrill
    Against its waiting window, open still!

II*

When from the blossoms of the noiseful day
  Unto the hive of sleep and hushèd gloom
Throng the dim-wingèd dreams—what dreams are they
  That with the wildest honey hover home?

* Both in its theme and in its imagery this sonnet was written as a variation of Mrs. Meynell's verses 'At Night.'

319

Oh, they that have from many thousand thoughts
 Stolen the strange sweet of ever-blossomy you,
A thousand fancies in fair-coloured knots
 Which you are inexhausted meadow to.
Ah, what sharp heathery honey, quick with pain,
 Do they bring home! It holds the night awake
To hear their lovely murmur in my brain;
 And Sleep's wings have a trouble for your sake.
  Day and you dawn together: for at end
  With the first light breaks the first thought—
   'My friend!'

III

O FRIEND, who mak'st that mis-spent word of 'friend'
 Sweet as the low note that a summer dove
Fondles in her warm throat! And shall it end,
 Because so swift on friend and friend broke love?
Lo, when all words to honour thee are spent,
 And flung a bold stave to the old bald Time
Telling him that he is too insolent
 Who thinks to rase thee from my heart or rhyme;
Whereof to one because thou life hast given,
 The other yet shall give a life to thee,
Such as to gain, the prowest swords have striven,
 And compassed weaker immortality:
  These spent, my heart not stinteth in her breast
  Her sweet 'Friend! friend!'—one note, and loves
   it best.

IV

No, no, it cannot be, it cannot be,
　　Because this love of close-affinèd friends
In its sweet sudden ambush toilèd me
　　So swift, that therefore all as swift it ends.
For swift it was, yet quiet as the birth
　　Of smoothest Music in a Master's soul,
Whose mild fans lapsing as she slides to earth
　　Waver in the bold arms which dare control
Her from her lineal heaven; yea, it was still
　　As the young Moon that bares her nightly breast,
And smiles to see the Babe earth suck its fill.
　　　O Halcyon! was thine auspice not of rest?
　　　　　Shall this proud verse bid after-livers see
　　　　　How friends could love for immortality?

V

When that part heavenliest of all-heavenly you
　　First at my side did breathe its blossomy air,
What lovely wilderment alarmed me through!
　　On what ambrosial effluence did I fare,
And comforts Paradisal! What gales came,
　　Through ports for one divinest space ajar,
Of rankèd lilies blown into a flame
　　By watered banks where walks of young Saints are!
One attent space, my trembling locks did rise
　　Swayed on the wind, in planetary wheel
Of intervolving sweet societies,
　　　From wavèd vesture and from fledgèd heel
　　　　　Odorous aspersion trailing. Then, alone
　　　　　In her eyes' ventral glory, God took throne.

TO A CHILD

WHENAS my Life shall time with funeral tread
    The heavy death-drum of the beaten hours,
Following, sole mourner, mine own manhood dead,
    Poor forgot corse, where not a maid strows flowers;
When I you love am no more I you love,
    But go with unsubservient feet, behold
Your dear face through changed eyes, all grim change
        prove;—
    A new man, mockèd with misname of old;
When shamed Love keeps his ruined lodging, elf!
    When, ceremented in mouldering memory,
Myself is hearsèd underneath myself,
    And I am but the monument of me:—
        O to that tomb be tender then, which bears
        Only the name of him it sepulchres!

HERMES

SOOTHSAY. Behold, with rod twy-serpented,
    Hermes the prophet, twining in one power
The woman with the man. Upon his head
    The cloudy cap, wherewith he hath in dower
The cloud's own virtue—change and counterchange,
    To show in light, and to withdraw in pall,
As mortal eyes best bear. His lineage strange
    From Zeus, Truth's sire, and maiden May—the all
Illusive Nature. His fledged feet declare
    That 'tis the nether self transdeified.

And the thrice-furnaced passions, which do bear
  The poet Olympusward. In him allied
      Both parents clasp; and from the womb of Nature
      Stern Truth takes flesh in shows of lovely feature.

HOUSE OF BONDAGE

I

When I perceive Love's heavenly reaping still
  Regard perforce the clouds' vicissitude,
That the fixed spirit loves not when it will,
  But craves its seasons of the flawful blood;
When I perceive that the high poet doth
  Oft voiceless stray beneath the uninfluent stars,
That even Urania of her kiss is loth,
  And Song's brave wings fret on their sensual bars;
When I perceive the fullest-sailèd sprite
  Lag at most need upon the lethèd seas,
The provident captainship oft voided quite,
  And lamèd lie deep-draughted argosies;
      I scorn myself, that put for such strange toys
      The wit of man to purposes of boys.

II

The spirit's ark sealed with a little clay
  Was old ere Memphis grew a memory;*
The hand pontifical to break away
  That seal what shall surrender? Not the sea
Which did englut great Egypt and his war,

Nor all the desert-drownèd sepulchres.
Love's feet are stained with clay and travel-sore,
　And dusty are Song's lucent wing and hairs.
O Love, that must do courtesy to decay,
　Eat hasty bread standing with loins up-girt,
How shall this stead thy feet for their sore way?
　Ah, Song, what brief embraces balm thy hurt!
　　Had Jacob's toil full guerdon, casting his
　　Twice-seven heaped years to burn in Rachel's kiss?

THE HEART

To my Critic who had objected to the phrase—
'The heart's burning floors.'

I

THE heart you hold too small and local thing
　Such spacious terms of edifice to bear.
And yet, since Poesy first shook out her wing,
　The mighty Love has been impalaced there;
That has she given him as his wide demesne,
　And for his sceptre ample empery;
Against its door to knock has Beauty been
　Content; it has its purple canopy,
A dais for the sovereign lady spread
　Of many a lover, who the heaven would think
Too low an awning for her sacred head.

* The Ark of the Egyptian temple was sealed with clay, which
the Pontiff-King broke when he entered the inner shrine to offer
worship.

The world, from star to sea, cast down its brink—
    Yet shall that chasm, till He Who these did build
    An awful Curtius make Him, yawn unfilled.

II

O NOTHING, in this corporal earth of man,
    That to the imminent heaven of his high soul
Responds with colour and with shadow, can
    Lack correlated greatness. If the scroll
Where thoughts lie fast in spell of hieroglyph
    Be mighty through its mighty habitants;
If God be in His Name; grave potence if
    The sounds unbind of hieratic chants;
All's vast that vastness means. Nay, I affirm
    Nature is whole in her least things exprest,
Nor know we with what scope God builds the worm.
    Our towns are copied fragments from our breast;
        And all man's Babylons strive but to impart
        The grandeurs of his Babylonion heart.

DESIDERIUM INDESIDERATUM

O GAIN that lurk'st ungainèd in all gain!
O love we just fall short of in all love!
O height that in all heights art still above!
O beauty that dost leave all beauty pain!
Thou unpossessed that mak'st possession vain,
See these strained arms which fright the simple air,
And say what ultimate fairness holds thee, Fair!
They girdle Heaven, and girdle Heaven in vain;

They shut, and lo! but shut in their unrest.
Thereat a voice in me that voiceless was:—
'Whom seekest thou through the unmarged arcane
And not discern'st to thine own bosom prest?'
I looked. My claspèd arms athwart my breast
Framed the august embraces of the Cross.

LOVE'S VARLETS

Love, he is nearer (though the moralist
    Of rule and line cry shame on me), more near
To thee and to the heart of thee, be't wist,
    Who sins against thee even for the dear
Lack that he hath of thee; than who, chill-wrapt
    In thy light-thought-on customed livery,
Keeps all thy laws with formal service apt,
    Save that great law to tremble and to be
Shook to his heart-strings if there do but pass
    The rumour of thy pinions. Such one is
Thy varlet, guerdoned with the daily mass
    That feed on thy remainder-meats of bliss.
        More hath he of thy bosom, whose slips of grace
        Fell through despair of thy close-gracious face.

NON PAX—EXPECTATIO

Hush! 'tis the gap between two lightnings. Room
Is none for peace in this thou callest peace,
This breathing-while wherein the breathings cease.
The pulses sicken, hearkening through the gloom.

Afar the thunders of a coming doom
Ramp on the cowering winds. Lo! at the dread,
Thy heart's tomb yawns and renders up its dead,—
The hopes 'gainst hope embalmèd in its womb.

Canst thou endure, if the pent flood o'erflows?
Who is estated heir to constancy?
Behold, I hardly know if I outlast
The minute underneath whose heel I lie;
Yet I endure, have stayed the minute passed,
Perchance may stay the next. Who knows, who knows?

NOT EVEN IN DREAM

THIS love is crueller than the other love:
    We had the Dreams for Tryst, we other pair;
But here there is no *we;*—not anywhere
    Returning breaths of sighs about me move.
No wings, even of the stuff which fancy wove,
    Perturb Sleep's air with a responsive flight
When mine sweep into dreams. My soul in fright
    Circles as round its widowed nest a dove.

One shadow but usurps another's place:
    And, though this shadow more enthralling is,
Alas, it hath no lips at all to miss!
    I have not even that former poignant bliss,
That haunting sweetness, that forlorn sad trace,
    The phantom memory of a vanished kiss.

MISCELLANEOUS POEMS

A HOLLOW WOOD

This is the mansion built for me
By the sweating centuries;
Roofed with intertwinèd tree,
Woofed with green for my princelier ease.
Here I lie with my world about me,
Shadowed off from the world without me,
Even as my thoughts embosom me
From wayside humanity.
And here can only enter who
Delight me—the unpricèd few.
Come you in, and make you cheer,
It draweth toward my banquet-time.
Would you win to my universe,
Your thoughts must turn in the wards of rhyme.
Loose the chain of linkèd verse,
Stoop your knowledge, and enter here!

Here cushioned ivies you invite
To fall to with appetite.
What for my viands?—Dainty thoughts.
What for my brows?—Forget-me-nots.
What for my feet?—A bath of green.
My servers?—Phantasies unseen.

What shall I find me for feasting dress?—
Your white disusèd childlikeness.
What hid music will laugh to my calls?—
An orgy of mad bird-bacchanals.
Such meat, such music, such coronals!
From the cask which the summer sets aflow
Under the roof of my raftered house,
The birds above, we below,
We carouse as they carouse.
Or have but the ear the ear within,
And you may hear, if you hold you mute,
You may hear by my amulet,
The wind-like keenness of violin,
The enamelled tone of shallow flute,
And the furry richness of clarinet.
These are the things shall make you cheer,
If you will grace my banquet-time.
Would you win to my universe,
Your thought must turn in the wards of rhyme.
Loose the chain of linkèd verse,
Stoop your knowledge, and enter here!

TO DAISIES

Ah, drops of gold in whitening flame
Burning, we know your lovely name—
Daisies, that little children pull!
Like all weak things, over the strong
Ye do not know your power for wrong,
And much abuse your feebleness.
Weak maids, with flutter of a dress,

Increase most heavy tyrannies;
And vengeance unto heaven cries
For multiplied injustice of dove-eyes.
Daises, that little children pull,
As ye are weak, be merciful!
O hide your eyes! they are to me
Beautiful insupportably.
Or be but conscious ye are fair,
And I your loveliness could bear;
But, being fair so without art,
Ye vex the silted memories of my heart!

As a pale ghost yearning strays
With sundered gaze,
'Mid corporal presences that are
To it impalpable—such a bar
Sets you more distant than the morning-star.
Such wonder is on you and amaze,
I look and marvel if I be
Indeed the phantom, or are ye?
The light is on your innocence
Which fell from me.
The fields ye still inhabit whence
My world-acquainted treading strays,
The country where I did commence;
And though ye shine to me so near,
So close to gross and visible sense,
Between us lies impassable year on year.
To other time and far-off place
Belongs your beauty: silent thus,
Though to others naught you tell,
To me your ranks are rumorous
Of an ancient miracle.

Vain does my touch your petals graze,
I touch you not; and, though ye blossom here,
Your roots are fast in alienated days.
Ye there are anchored, while Time's stream
Has swept me past them: your white ways
And infantile delights do seem
To look in on me like a face.
Dead and sweet, come back through dream,
With tears, because for old embrace
It has no arms. These hands did toy,
Children, with you when I was child,
And in each other's eyes we smiled:
Not yours, not yours the grievous-fair
Apparelling
With which you wet mine eyes; you wear,
Ah me, the garment of the grace
I wove you when I was a boy;
O mine, and not the year's, your stolen Spring!
And since ye wear it,
Hide your sweet selves! I cannot bear it.
For, when ye break the cloven earth
With your young laughter and endearment,
No blossomy carillon 'tis of mirth
To me; I see my slaughtered joy
Bursting its cerement.

TO THE SINKING SUN

How graciously thou wear'st the yoke
    Of use that does not fail!
The grasses, like an anchored smoke,

Ride in the bending gale;
This knoll is snowed with blosmy manna,
    And fire-dropt as a seraph's mail.

Here every eve thou stretchest out
    Untarnishable wing,
And marvellously bring'st about
    Newly an olden thing;
Nor ever through like-ordered heaven
    Moves largely thy grave progressing.

Here every eve thou goest down
    Behind the self-same hill,
Nor ever twice alike go'st down
    Behind the self-same hill;
Nor like-ways is one flame-sopped flower
    Possessed with glory past its will.

Not twice alike! I am not blind,
    My sight is live to see;
And yet I do complain of thy
    Weary variety.
O Sun! I ask thee less or more,
    Change not at all, or utterly!

O give me unprevisioned new,
    Or give to change reprieve!
For new in me is olden too,
    That I for sameness grieve.
O flowers! O grasses! be but once
    The grass and flower of yester-eve!

Wonder and sadness are the lot
    Of change: thou yield'st mine eyes
Grief of vicissitude, but not
    Its penetrant surprise.
Immutability mutable
    Burthens my spirit and the skies.

O altered joy, all joyed of yore,
    Plodding in unconned ways!
O grief grieved out, and yet once more
    A dull, new, staled amaze!
I dream, and all was dreamed before,
    Or dream I so? the dreamer says.

A MAY BURDEN

THROUGH meadow-ways as I did tread,
The corn grew in great lustihead,
And hey! the beeches burgeonèd.
    By Goddès fay, by Goddès fay!
It is the month, the jolly month,
It is the jolly month of May.

God ripe the wines and corn, I say,
And wenches for the marriage-day,
And boys to teach love's comely play.
    By Goddès fay, by Goddès fay!
It is the month, the jolly month,
It is the jolly month of May.

As I went down by lane and lea,
The daisies reddened so, pardie!
'Blushets!' I said, 'I well do see,
    By Goddès fay, by Goddès fay!
The thing ye think of in this month,
Heigho! this jolly month of May.'

As down I went by rye and oats,
The blossoms smelt of kisses; throats
Of birds turned kisses into notes;
    By Goddès fay, by Goddès fay!
The kiss it is a growing flower,
I trow, this jolly month of May!

God send a mouth to every kiss,
Seeing the blossom of this bliss
By gathering doth grow, certes!
    By Goddès fay, by Goddès fay!
Thy brow-garland pushed all aslant
Tells—but I tell not, wanton May!

  The first two stanzas are from a French original—I have for-
gotten what.

JULY FUGITIVE

CAN you tell me where has hid her
    Pretty Maid July?
I would swear one day ago
    She passed by,
I would swear that I do know
    The blue bliss of her eye:

'Tarry, maid, maid,' I bid her;
    But she hastened by.
Do you know where she has hid her,
    Maid July?

Yet in truth it needs must be
    The flight of her is old;
Yet in truth it needs must be,
    For her nest, the earth, is cold.
No more in the poolèd Even
    Wade her rosy feet,
Dawn-flakes no more plash from them
    To poppies 'mid the wheat.
She has muddied the day's oozes
    With her petulant feet;
Scared the clouds that floated,
    As sea-birds they were,
Slow on the cœrule
    Lulls of the air,
Lulled on the luminous
    Levels of air:
She has chidden in a pet
    All her stars from her;
Now they wander loose and sigh
    Through the turbid blue,
Now they wander, weep, and cry—
    Yea, and I too—
'Where are you, sweet July,
    Where are you?'

Who hath beheld her footprints,
  Or the pathway she goes?
Tell me, wind, tell me, wheat?
  Which of you knows?
Sleeps she swathed in the flushed Arctic
  Night of the rose?
Or lie her limbs like Alp-glow
  On the lily's snows?
Gales, that are all-visitant,
  Find the runaway;
And for him who findeth her
  (I do charge you say)
I will throw largesse of broom
  Of this summer's mintage,
I will broach a honey-bag
  Of the bee's best vintage.
Breezes, wheat, flowers sweet,
  None of them knows!
How then shall we lure her back
  From the way she goes?
For it were a shameful thing,
  Saw we not this comer
Ere Autumn camp upon the fields
  Red with rout of Summer.

When the bird quits the cage,
  We set the cage outside,
With seed and with water,
  And the door wide,
Haply we may win it so
  Back to abide.
Hang her cage of Earth out

O'er Heaven's sunward wall,
Its four gates open, winds in watch
By reinèd cars at all;
Relume in hanging hedgerows
The rain-quenched blossom,
And roses sob their tears out
On the gale's warm heaving bosom;
Shake the lilies till their scent
Over-drip their rims;
That our runaway may see
We do know her whims:
Sleek the tumbled waters out
For her travelled limbs;
Strew and smooth blue night thereon:
There will—O not doubt her!—
The lovely sleepy lady lie,
With all her stars about her!

FIELD-FLOWER

A PHANTASY

God took a fit of Paradise-wind,
A slip of cœrule weather,
A thought as simple as Himself,
And ravelled them together.
Unto His eyes He held it there,
To teach it gazing debonair
With memory of what, perdie,
A God's young innocences were.
His fingers pushed it through the sod—

It came up redolent of God,
Garrulous of the eyes of God
    To all the breezes near it;
Musical of the mouth of God
    To all had ears to hear it;
Mystical with the mirth of God,
    That glow-like did ensphere it.
        And—'Babble! babble! babble!' said;
        'I'll tell the whole world one day!'
        There was no blossom half so glad,
        Since sun of Christ's first Sunday.

A poet took a flaw of pain.
    A hap of skiey pleasure,
A thought had in his cradle lain,
    And mingled them in measure.
That chrism he laid upon his eyes,
And lips, and heart, for euphrasies,
    That he might see, feel, sing, perdie,
The simple things that are the wise.
Beside the flower he held his ways,
And leaned him to it gaze for gaze—
He took its meaning, gaze for gaze,
    As baby looks on baby;
Its meaning passed into his gaze,
    Native as meaning may be;
He rose with all his shining gaze
    As children's eyes at play be.
        And—'Babble! babble! babble!' said;
        'I'll tell the whole world one day!'
        There was no poet half so glad,
        Since man grew God that Sunday.

TO A SNOWFLAKE

WHAT heart could have thought you?—
Past our devisal
(O filigree petal!)
Fashioned so purely,
Fragilely, surely,
From what Paradisal
Imagineless metal,
Too costly for cost?
Who hammered you, wrought you,
From argentine vapour?—
'God was my shaper.
Passing surmisal,
He hammered, He wrought me,
From curled silver vapour,
To lust of His mind:—
Thou could'st not have thought me!
So purely, so palely,
Tinily, surely,
Mightily, frailly,
Insculped and embossed,
With His hammer of wind,
And His graver of frost.'

A QUESTION

O BIRD with heart of wassail,
    That toss the Bacchic branch,
And slip your shaken music,
    An elfin avalanche;

Come tell me, O tell me,
  My poet of the blue!
What's *your* thought of me, Sweet?—
  Here's *my* thought of you.

A small thing, a wee thing,
  A brown fleck of naught;
With winging and singing
  That who could have thought?

A small thing, a wee thing,
  A brown amaze withal,
That fly a pitch more azure
  Because you're so small.

Bird, I'm a small thing—
  My angel descries;
With winging and singing
  That who could surmise?

Ah, small things, ah, wee things,
  Are the poets all,
Whose tour's the more azure
  Because they're so small.

The angels hang watching
  The tiny men-things:—
'The dear speck of flesh, see,
  With such daring wings!

'Come, tell us, O tell us,
    Thou strange mortality!
What's *thy* thought of us, Dear?—
    Here's *our* thought of thee.'

'Alack! you tall angels,
    I can't think so high!
I can't think what it feels like
    Not to be I.'

Come tell me, O tell me,
    My poet of the blue!
What's *your* thought of me, Sweet?—
    Here's *my* thought of you.

THE CLOUD'S SWAN-SONG

THERE is a parable in the pathless cloud,
There's prophecy in heaven,—they did not lie,
The Chaldee shepherds,—sealèd from the proud,
To cheer the weighted heart that mates the seeing eye.

A lonely man, oppressed with lonely ills,
And all the glory fallen from my song,
Here do I walk among the windy hills;
The wind and I keep both one monotoning tongue.

Like grey clouds one by one my songs upsoar
Over my soul's cold peaks; and one by one
They loose their little rain, and are no more;
And whether well or ill, to tell me there is none.

For 'tis an alien tongue, of alien things,
From all men's care, how miserably apart!
Even my friends say: 'Of what is this he sings?'
And barren is my song, and barren is my heart.

For who can work, unwitting his work's worth?
Better, meseems, to know the work for naught,
Turn my sick course back to the kindly earth,
And leave to ampler plumes the jetting tops of thought.

And visitations that do often use
Remote, unhappy, inauspicious sense
Of doom, and poets widowed of their muse,
And what dark 'gan, dark ended, in me did commence.

I thought of spirit wronged by mortal ills,
And my flesh rotting on my fate's dull stake;
And how self-scornèd they the bounty fills
Of others, and the bread, even of their dearest, take.

I thought of Keats, that died in perfect time,
In predecease of his just-sickening song;
Of him that set, wrapt in his radiant rhyme,
Sunlike in sea. Life longer had been life too long.

But I, exanimate of quick Poesy,—
O then no more but even a soulless corse!
Nay, my Delight dies not; 'tis I should be
Her dead, a stringless harp on which she had no force.

Of my wild lot I thought; from place to place,
Apollo's song-bowed Scythian, I go on;
Making in all my home, with pliant ways,
But, provident of change, putting forth root in none.

Now, with starved brain, sick body, patience galled
With fardels even to wincing; from fair sky
Fell sudden little rain, scarce to be called
A shower, which of the instant was gone wholly by.

What cloud thus died I saw not; heaven was fair.
Methinks my angel plucked my locks: I bowed
My spirit, shamed; and looking in the air:—
'Even so,' I said, 'even so, my brother the good Cloud?'

It was a pilgrim of the fields of air,
Its home was allwheres the wind left it rest,
And in a little forth again did fare,
And in all places was a stranger and a guest.

It harked all breaths of heaven, and did obey
With sweet peace their uncomprehended wills;
It knew the eyes of stars which made no stay,
And with the thunder walked upon the lonely hills.

And from the subject earth it seemed to scorn,
It drew the sustenance whereby it grew
Perfect in bosom for the married Morn,
And of his life and light full as a maid kissed new.

Its also darkness of the face withdrawn,
And the long waiting for the little light,
So long in life so little. Like a fawn
It fled with tempest breathing hard at heel of flight;

And having known full East, did not disdain
To sit in shadow and oblivious cold,
Save what all loss doth of its loss retain,
And who hath held hath somewhat that he still must hold.

Right poet! who thy rightness to approve,
Having all liberty, didst keep all measure,
And with a firmament for ranging, move
But at the heavens' uncomprehended pleasure.

With amplitude unchecked, how sweetly thou
Didst wear the ancient custom of the skies,
And yoke of used prescription; and thence how
Find gay variety no license could devise!

As we the quested beauties better wit
Of the one grove our own than forests great,
Restraint, by the delighted search of it,
Turns to right scope. For lovely moving intricate

Is put to fair devising in the curb
Of ordered limit; and all-changeful Hermes
Is Terminus as well. Yet we perturb
Our souls for latitude, whose strength in bound and
    term is.

How far am I from heavenly liberty,
That play at policy with change and fate,
Who should my soul from foreign broils keep free,
In the fast-guarded frontiers of its single state!

Could I face firm the Is, and with To-be
Trust Heaven; to Heaven commit the deed, and do;
In power contained, calm in infirmity,
And fit myself to change with virtue ever new;

Thou hadst not shamed me, cousin of the sky,
Thou wandering kinsman, that didst sweetly live
Unnoted, and unnoted sweetly die,
Weeping more gracious song than any I can weave;

Which these gross-tissued words do sorely wrong.
Thou hast taught me on powerlessness a power;
To make song wait on life, not life on song;
To hold sweet not too sweet, and bread for bread though
    sour;

By law to wander, to be strictly free.
With tears ascended from the heart's sad sea,
Ah, such a silver song to Death could I
Sing, Pain would list, forgetting Pain to be,
And Death would tarry marvelling, and forget to die!

OF MY FRIEND

THE moonlight cloud of her invisible beauty,
    Shook from the torrent glory of her soul
In aëry spray, hangs round her; love grows duty,

If you that angel-populous aureole
    Have the glad power to feel;
      As all our longings kneel
To the intense and cherub-wingèd stole
Orbing a painted Saint: and through control
      Of this sweet faint
      Veil, my unguessing Saint
Celestial ministrations sheds which heal.

           *   *   *   *

Now, Friend, short sweet outsweetening sharpest woes!
    In wintry cold a little, little flame—
So much to me that little!—here I close
    This errant song. O pardon its much blame!
      Now my grey day grows bright
      A little ere the night;
Let after-livers who may love my name,
And gauge the price I paid for dear-bought fame,
      Know that at end,
      Pain was well paid, sweet Friend,
Pain was well paid which brought me to your sight.

TO MONICA: AFTER NINE YEARS

    In the land of flag-lilies,
    Where burst in golden clangours
    The joy-bells of the broom,
    You were full of willy-nillies,
    Pets, and bee-like angers:
    Flaming like a dusky poppy,
    In a wrathful bloom.

You were full of sweet and sour,
Like a dish of strawberries
Set about with curd.
In your petulant foot was power
In your wilful innocences,
Your wild and fragrant word.
O, was it you that sweetly spake
Or I that sweetly heard?

Yellow were the wheat-ways,
The poppies were most red;
And all your meet and feat ways
Your sudden bee-like snarlings,—
Ah, do you remember,
Darling of the darlings?
Or is it but an ember,
A rusted peal of joy-bells,
Their golden buzzings dead?

Now at one, and now at two,
Swift to pout and swift to woo,
The maid I knew:
Still I see the duskèd tresses—
But the old angers, old caresses?
Still your eyes are autumn thunders,
But where are you, child, you?

This your beauty is a script
Writ with pencil brightest-dipt—
Oh, it is the fairest scroll
For a young, departed soul!—
Thus you say:

'Thrice three years ago to-day,
There was one
Shall no more beneath the sun
Darkle, fondle, featly play.
If to think on her be gloom,
Rejoice she has so rich a tomb!'

But there's he—
Ask thou not who it may be!—
That, until Time's boughs are bare,
Shall be unconsoled for her.

A DOUBLE NEED

(To W—)

AH, gone the days when for undying kindness
I still could render you undying song!
You yet can give, but I can give no more;
Fate, in her extreme blindness,
Has wrought me so great wrong.
I am left poor indeed;
Gone is my sole and amends-making store,
And I am needy with a double need.

Behold that I am like a fountained nymph,
Lacking her customed lymph,
The longing parched in stone upon her mouth,
Unwatered of its ancient plenty. She
(Remembering her irrevocable streams),
A Thirst made marble, sits perpetually
With sundered lips of still-memorial drouth.

GRIEF'S HARMONICS

At evening, when the lank and rigid trees,
To the mere forms of their sweet day-selves drying,
On heaven's blank leaf seem pressed and flattenèd;
Or rather, to my sombre thoughts replying,
Of plumes funereal the thin effigies;
That hour when all old dead things seem most dead,
And their death instant most and most undying,
That the flesh aches at them; there stirred in me
The babe of an unborn calamity,
Ere its due time to be deliverèd.
Dead sorrow and sorrow unborn so blent their pain,
That which more present was were hardly said,
But both more *now* than any Now can be.
My soul like sackcloth did her body rend,
And thus with Heaven contend:—
'Let pass the chalice of this coming dread,
Or that fore-drained O bid me not re-drain!'
So have I asked, who know my asking vain;
Woe against woe in antiphon set over,
That grief's soul transmigrates, and lives again,
And in new pang old pang's incarnatèd.

MEMORAT MEMORIA

Come you living or dead to me, out of the silt of the Past,
With the sweet of the piteous first, and the shame of the
    shameful last?
Come with your dear and dreadful face through the passes
    of Sleep,
The terrible mask, and the face it masked—the face you did
   not keep?

You are neither two nor one—I would you were one or
two,

For your awful self is embalmed in the fragrant self I
knew:

And Above may ken, and Beneath may ken, what I mean by
these words of whirl,

But by my sleep that sleepeth not,—O Shadow of a Girl!—

Naught here but I and my dreams shall know the secret
of this thing:—

For ever the songs I sing are sad with the songs I never
sing,

Sad are sung songs, but how more sad the songs we dare
not sing!

Ah, the ill that we do in tenderness, and the hateful horror
of love!

It has sent more souls to the unslaked Pit than it ever
will draw above.

I damned you, girl, with my pity, who had better by far
been thwart,

And drave you hard on the track to hell, because I was
gentle of heart.

I shall have no comfort now in scent, no ease in dew, for
this;

I shall be afraid of daffodils, and rose-buds are amiss;

You have made a thing of innocence as shameful as a sin,

I shall never feel a girl's soft arms without horror of the
skin.

My child! what was it that I sowed, that I so ill should
reap?

You have done this to me. And I, what I to you?—It lies
with Sleep.

NOCTURN

I WALK, I only,
Not I only wake;
Nothing is, this sweet night,
But doth couch and wake
For its love's sake;
Everything, this sweet night,
Couches with its mate.
For whom but for the stealthy-visitant sun
Is the naked moon
Tremulous and elate?
The heaven hath the earth
Its own and all apart;
The hushèd pool holdeth
A star to its heart.
You may think the rose sleepeth,
But though she folded is,
The wind doubts her sleeping;
Not all the rose sleeps,
But smiles in her sweet heart
For crafty bliss.
The wind lieth with the rose,
And when he stirs, she stirs in her repose:
The wind hath the rose,
And the rose her kiss.
Ah, mouth of me!
Is it then that this
Seemeth much to thee?—
I wander only.
The rose hath her kiss.

HEAVEN AND HELL

'Tis said there were no thought of hell,
 Save hell were taught; that there should be
A Heaven for all's self-credible.
 Not so the thing appears to me.
'Tis Heaven that lies beyond our sights,
 And hell too possible that proves;
For all can feel the God that smites,
 But ah, how few the God that loves!

'CHOSE VUE'

A Metrical Caprice

Up she rose, fair daughter—well she was graced,
As a cloud her going, stept from her chair,
As a summer-soft cloud in her going paced,
Down dropped her riband-band, and all her waving hair
Shook like loosened music cadent to her waist;—
Lapsing like music, wavery as water,
 Slid to her waist.

ST MONICA

At the Cross thy station keeping
With the mournful Mother weeping,
Thou, unto the sinless Son,
Weepest for thy sinful one.
Blood and water from His side

Gush; in thee the streams divide:
From thine eyes the one doth start,
But the other from thy heart.

Mary, for thy sinner, see,
To her Sinless mourns with thee;
Could that Son the son not heed,
For whom two such mothers plead?
So thy child had baptism twice,
And the whitest from thine eyes.

The floods lift up, lift up their voice,
With a many-watered noise!
Down the centuries fall those sweet
Sobbing waters to our feet,
And our laden air still keeps
Murmur of a Saint that weeps.

Teach us but, to grace our prayers,
Such divinity of tears,—
Earth should be lustrate again
With contrition of that rain:
Till celestial floods o'er-rise
The high tops of Paradise.

MARRIAGE IN TWO MOODS

I

LOVE that's loved from day to day
Loves itself unto decay:
He that eats one daily fruit

Shrivels hunger at the root.
Daily pleasure grows a task;
Daily smiles become a mask.
Daily growth of unpruned strength
Expands to feebleness at length.
Daily increase thronging fast
Must devour itself at last.
Daily shining, even content
Would with itself grow discontent;
And the sun's life witnesseth
Daily dying is not death.
So Love loved from day to day
Loves itself into decay.

II

Love to daily uses wed
Shall be sweetly perfected.
Life by repetition grows
Unto its appointed close:
Day to day fulfils one year—
Shall not Love by Love wax dear?
All piles by repetition rise—
Shall not then Love's edifice?
Shall not Love, too, learn his writ,
Like Wisdom, by repeating it?
By the oft-repeated use
All perfections gain their thews;
And so, with daily uses wed,
Love, too, shall be perfected.

ALL FLESH

I DO not need the skies'
Pomp, when I would be wise;
For pleasaunce nor to use
Heaven's champaign when I muse.
One grass-blade in its veins
Wisdom's whole flood contains:
Thereon my foundering mind
Odyssean fate can find.

O little blade. now vaunt
Thee, and be arrogant!
Tell the proud sun that he
Sweated in shaping thee;
Night, that she did unvest
Her mooned and argent breast
To suckle thee. Heaven fain
Yearned over thee in rain,
And with wide parent wing
Shadowed thee, nested thing,
Fed thee, and slaved for thy
Impotent tyranny.
Nature's broad thews bent
Meek for thy content.
Mastering littleness
Which the wise heavens confess,
The fraility which doth draw
Magnipotence to its law—
These were, O happy one, these
Thy laughing puissances!
Be confident of thought,
Seeing that thou art naught;

And be thy pride thou'rt all
Delectably safe and small.
Epitomized in thee
Was the mystery
Which shakes the spheres conjoint—
God focussed to a point.

All thy fine mouths shout
Scorn upon dull-eyed doubt.
Impenetrable fool
Is he thou canst not school
To the humility
By which the angels see!
Unfathomably framed
Sister, I am not shamed
Before the cherubin
To vaunt my flesh thy kin.
My one hand thine, and one
Imprisoned in God's own,
I am as God; alas,
And such a god of grass!
A little root clay-caught,
A wind, a flame, a thought,
Inestimably naught!

THE KINGDOM OF GOD

'In no Strange Land'

O WORLD invisible, we view thee,
O world intangible, we touch thee,
O world unknowable, we know thee,
Inapprehensible, we clutch thee!

Does the fish soar to find the ocean,
The eagle plunge to find the air—
That we ask of the stars in motion
If they have rumour of thee there?

Not where the wheeling systems darken,
And our benumbed conceiving soars!—
The drift of pinions, would we hearken,
Beats at our own clay-shuttered doors.

The angels keep their ancient places;—
Turn but a stone, and start a wing!
'Tis ye, 'tis your estrangèd faces,
That miss the many-splendoured thing.

But (when so sad thou canst not sadder)
Cry;—and upon thy so sore loss
Shall shine the traffic of Jacob's ladder
Pitched betwixt Heaven and Charing Cross.

Yea, in the night, my Soul, my daughter,
Cry,—clinging Heaven by the hems;
And lo, Christ walking on the water
Not of Gennesareth, but Thames!

THE SINGER SAITH OF HIS SONG

THE touches of man's modern speech
    Perplex her unacquainted tongue;
There seems through all her songs a sound
    Of falling tears. She is not young.

Within her eyes' profound arcane
    Resides the glory of her dreams;
Behind her secret cloud of hair.
    She sees the Is beyond the Seems.

Her heart sole-towered in her steep spirit,
    Somewhat sweet is she, somewhat wan;
And she sings the songs of Sion
    By the streams of Babylon.

Modern Library of the World's Best Books

COMPLETE LIST OF TITLES IN

THE MODERN LIBRARY

For convenience in ordering use number at right of title

MODERN LIBRARY GIANTS

A series of full-sized library editions of books that formerly were available only in cumbersome and expensive sets.

THE MODERN LIBRARY GIANTS REPRESENT A SELECTION OF THE WORLD'S GREATEST BOOKS

Many are illustrated and some of them are over 1200 pages long.